MEMORIALS

OF

ST. ANN'S CHURCH,

MANCHESTER,

In the Last Century:

AN ATTEMPT TO RECTIFY SEVERAL POPULAR ERRORS;

TO WHICH IS ADDED A SHORT

HISTORY OF CHURCH BUILDING AND SUNDAY SCHOOL WORK

IN THE SAME TOWN.

BY

CHARLES WAREING BARDSLEY, M.A.

(Author of "English Surnames.")

MANCHESTER:

THOMAS ROWORTH, 21, ST. ANN'S SQUARE.

LONDON: SIMPKIN, MARSHALL, AND CO.

—

1877.

TO THE

RECTOR, CHURCHWARDENS, AND CONGREGATION

OF

ST. ANN'S CHURCH, MANCHESTER:

THIS LITTLE

𝕸𝖊𝖒𝖔𝖗𝖎𝖆𝖑

OF A

SANCTUARY BELOVED AND FREQUENTED BY THEM

IS DEDICATED.

CONTENTS.

PREFACE.

THE purpose of this short history is primarily to correct one or two popular errors. One is but slight, and concerns an individual. The late Dr. Halley, in his "History of Lancashire Nonconformity," a book deserving the highest praise for its general accuracy of fact, and its charity of spirit, would lead the reader to suppose that the rectors and church-wardens of St. Ann's, like their congregations, were all at one in their hatred of Jacobitism, and their hostility to the Collegiate Chapter, and that there were positively no relations whatever subsisting between the Old and the New Church during the first half of the eighteenth century. This somewhat inaccurate view is modified by the facts herein related. Another, and far more curious, error is of an opposite character. An impression prevails among hundreds of our townspeople that St. Ann's was a hot-bed of Jacobitism, and that it was the Sanctuary of the Non-Jurors.

A writer the other day—and he is not the only one who has so written—spoke of St. Ann's as "that famous Non-Juring

Church." Between Dr. Halley and this gentleman what are we to believe? To modify a slight exaggeration, and to correct a falsehood, is the main purpose of the following chapters.

I need not say my little book is not intended for the Antiquarian. Some of the facts may possibly be new to him, for the simple reason that there are documents which have materially assisted me, to which he could not have obtained access. But any diligent frequenter of our noble Chetham Library can obtain all the information I have put together; and I dare say that such splendid representatives of local research as Mr. Crossley or Canon Raines, or such a student of mortuary registers as Mr. Owen, could have gleaned yet more facts than I have been able to state.

The narrative will at times, I fear, read brokenly; for this I must throw myself on the clemency of the reader. I have not had time to write carefully, or revise exactly. I have, however, tried to write popularly, as I have had to deal with popular mistakes.

Although the political history of St. Ann's terminated soon after Archdeacon Ward's appointment, I have carried on the story to the end of his life, as it gave me an opportunity of showing how the building of churches increased in Manchester towards the close of the last century, and of pointing out the causes and the influences that brought about their erection.

A short review of the history of Sunday Schools in Manchester is added; one or two popular errors are also rectified there. It is quite possible I may have fallen into errors myself. I shall be pleased if any reader will point them out to me.

I am glad to take this opportunity of stating how utterly impossible it would have been for me to complete these Memorials without the aid of the Chetham Library, and especially the publications of the Chetham Society, which have been edited by such men in the past as Canon Parkinson and Mr. Harland, and in the present as Canon Raines and Mr. Crossley. A series of works have been put forth which have brought to light many interesting facts concerning political and social life in Manchester, which otherwise must have been buried in uncertainty, if not obscurity. The occasional references to our town in the general works of the time are of no assistance to the antiquarian. The "General Gazetteer" of 1791, which is stated in the preface to have been "improved with additions and corrections," gravely supplies the following piece of information respecting Manchester :—" Its chief ornaments are the College, the Market Place, and the Collegiate Church, which last has a small choir of exquisite workmanship. It has an additional church, which was begun in Queen Anne's reign, and finished in 1723." According to this statement, St. Ann's was fifteen years in building, instead of four. But that is a trifling error compared to the wholesale omission of such churches as St. Mary's, St. John's, St. Paul's, St. James', and St. Michael's. There were seven churches, at least, in the town in 1791. This same "General Gazetteer" utterly ignores the existence of Liverpool! Yet its avowed purpose was to give an account of every notable town, village, or hamlet in England. Certainly Liverpool is a mushroom community, but it had unmistakably a local habitation and a name in 1791 ! I may add that this same publication dismisses the Manchester manufacturers in a single line by declaring that " their velvets of late are come into great repute, and are made much use of for breeches,"—nothing else ! After this we may be thankful for the Chetham Society.

I have to record my obligations to Mr. Richard Wood, and also to Mr. John Scholes, for the loan of several old Hymn Books printed for the use of St. Ann's congregation in 1784, 1790, and 1809 (*vide* Appendix III.) ; to Mr. Edmund Mason for a Report of the Manchester Church Schools from 1805 to 1810 ; and to the Rev. William Marshall, Rector of St. Paul's, for several documents relating to the large schools now under his own supervision. The mainstays of my paper on the Sunday School system, however, have been the Reports of the Committee, which lie in the Chetham Library, and the occasional allusions found in the *Mercury*. Often mingled up with advertisements, or hidden in a corner, these allusions are hard to discover. But patience and determination will be amply rewarded in this as in every other labour.

Mr. J. E. Bailey has kindly called my attention to a letter in the *Guardian's* Notes and Queries (April 24th, 1876) by C. S., in answer to a query propounded by Mr. Bailey himself, concerning the alleged likeness (*vide* p. 13) between St. Ann's, Manchester, and St. Andrew's, Holborn. C. S. writes, " Having been accustomed, during the last twenty years on my visits to London, to attend the church of St. Andrew, Holborn, I feel sure that it was the model from which St. Ann's was built. St. Ann's is St. Andrew's with the galleries squeezed nearer together and the length somewhat shortened, but the thickness of the pillars, and depth of the gallery front, not much, if at all, reduced. I suspect St. Andrew's would as nearly as possible cover the whole of St. Ann's churchyard within the palisades. It is, I have often thought, one of Sir Christopher Wren's best specimens of a church for a crowded neighbourhood, as Holborn must have been even two hundred years ago. . . . . I have often thought, and said, that it is surprising our Church architects in Manchester have never suggested an adaptation of St. Ann's for districts where large numbers of people have to be brought within reach of the preacher's voice." I fear C. S. will have to wait a long time before he sees any more St. Ann's Churches erected. Modern ecclesiastic taste is utterly against them. Nevertheless, Manchester was very proud of her second Church in the last century, and "beautiful," "sumptuous," and such like terms were freely heaped upon it. Within a few days of the consecration of the Church, Mr. Newcome, rector of Middleton, dedicating a sermon (preached in Manchester at the Triennial Visitation of Sir William Dawes) to his Diocesan, says: " One circumstance it may not be im-

proper here to take notice of, that at the same time your lordship came to Manchester upon your Visitation, you consecrated
a new Church, built there by the pious contributions of the
inhabitants, and some neighbouring benefactors : For the men-
tioning of this may be a publick vindication of that town, from
the sin I therein so freely declaimed against : As that beautiful
structure is a monument of their piety, and a standing evidence
how much they love and honour our order." *

* From this it appears the Visitation was held in the new Church.
This was exactly two days after the Consecration. The sermon is entitled :
"A Serious Admonition to all Despisers of the Clergy. In a Sermon
preached before the Right Rev. Father in God, William, Lord Bishop of
Chester, at his Triennial Visitation held at Manchester, in the County
Palatine of Lancaster, July 19, 1712. By Henry Newcome, A.M., rector
of Middleton, in Lancashire. The second edition. London : Printed for
Robert Scolfield, bookseller, in Rochdale ; and Sold by John Wyat, in
St. Paul's Churchyard, 1713." In Baines's "Lancashire" Henry New-
come is omitted in the list of Middleton's rectors. The order there is
" Robert Simmonds, 1663-1714. Samuel Sidebottom, 1714-1752." Henry
Newcome will come between the two. Sidebottom preached at St. Ann's
in 1714, as rector of Middleton, so Newcome's tenure must be subtracted
from Simmonds's.

proper here to take notice of, that at the same time your lordship came to Manchester upon your Visitation, you consecrated
a new Church, built there by the pious contributions of the
inhabitants, and some neighbouring benefactors : For the men-
tioning of this may be a publick vindication of that town, from
the sin I therein so freely declaimed against : As that beautiful

Page 1, line 4, for "*lucus non*" read "*lucus a non*."

Page 2 *(note)* for "100" read "140."

Page 10, line 14, for "Sir Thomas" read "Sir Tonman."

Page 52, line 17, for "wakes" read "waits."

Page 100, bottom line, for "refutation" read "attestation."

Memorials.

I.

THE PARISH OF ST. ANN'S.

HE occasional visitor to Manchester will speedily learn that Piccadilly, Market-street, the Market Place, and St. Ann's Square are the centre, if a line, and a crooked line withal, can be called a centre, of the city. The *lucus non lucendo* principle seems strong in these terms of local nomenclature, the market being conspicuous by its absence. If report speak truly the principle may seem, in the lapse of a few years, to have been carried to its furthest limit, for St. Ann's Square may possibly convey to the then casual wayfarer a dim impression that as the square is so termed because it is oblong, so the dedication is attached to it because no trace of feminine saintship is apparent. If rumour be correct, St. Ann's Church is to come down.

When the day of demolition arrives there will have disappeared not only a local landmark, but an historic record—a record not so much of the part itself has played, as of the drama it has witnessed. He who has looked on at battles, as well as he who has fought them, can give a narration of the conflict. What should we have done if we had not had men to chronicle history as well as to create it? With respect to

B

local affairs, St. Ann's has both chronicled and created matter of no little interest.   There are reminiscences, too, which are wholly her own.

The present boundaries of St. Ann's Parish are Market-street, St. Mary's Gate, Deansgate, Brasenose-street, Albert Square, Princess-street, Mosley-street, and Piccadilly.

A little more than two centuries ago, say about the date of the Commonwealth, the whole of this property was comprised of meadow land.   A single mansion, Radcliffe Hall, whose owner, Captain Robert Radcliffe, so bravely resisted the attacks of the Royalists but a few years previously, gave life to the scene.   Enclosed in its own demesnes, it stood on the rising ground above the present Unitarian Chapel in Cross-street.   Some rows of cottages, with projecting gables, well lathed and plastered, lined Market-street Lane from the present Brown-street, downwards to the crooked alley that led into Acres Field, now the Square.   Another batch of small tenements skirted the Deansgate side for one or two hundred yards. Till nigh the end of the seventeenth century, this represented the population of the future parish, ecclesiastically assigned to St. Ann's Church.

Since that period a population, varying from three to four thousand, has settled and fled.   It is strange but true that at this moment the number of residents within the boundary described is about the same as was found there in the days of Cromwell.*   The place is again, for at least one day in seven, a solitude, but not the solitude of meadows and hedgerows.   The primeval stillness of a desert isle is not, to my mind, so singularly lonesome as that silence of death where life has been.   Who will compare the stillness of the desert

* In 1838 there were no less than 200 people *resident* in St. Ann's Square and St. Ann's-street.   Probably not more than 100 now sleep within the whole parish boundaries; certainly not that number between Saturday and Monday.

sands to that of the city Tadmor which those sands surround ?
To strike out even now on the Sabbath from Cross-street, to
penetrate the narrow alleys and streetlets, and to thread one's
way into Mosley-street or Piccadilly, say about 11 o'clock in
the morning, is to feel a sensation not easily described.   From
Saturday night until cockcrowing on Monday morn, St. Ann's
parish is the true necropolis of commerce—rather, I should
say, its cemetery, for of its consols, its stocks, its choppings, and
changes, it may truly be said, "they are not dead, but sleeping,"—a sleep less protracted, if not less still, than that of the
God's-acre attached to the sanctuary nigh at hand ; for the
resurrection of Monday will quickly come again, and—then the
figure breaks down—then passion and greed will be resurrection-
ised too, and assert their sway over the seething human life
that has already peopled again the burial yard of merchandise.

He who looks upon the somewhat dimmed splendours of
the exterior fabric of St. Ann's, in Manchester, or St. Peter's,
in Liverpool, or St. Philip's, in Birmingham, may find in none
much to engage reflection or sentiment, and yet it is the
consecration of the first in 1712, of the second in 1704, and
of the third at the commencement of the eighteenth century,
that strikes the key-note of vicissitude in each of these great
towns.   Each marks the birth of that industrial life which at
first, beating but languidly, now throbs so like a mighty heart
that the most distant parts of the world feel, and are compelled
to feel, its pulsations ; each registered to the world the nativity
of the child-giant Commerce.

How correctly the building of churches gauges the spread
of manufacturing industry, and consequent growth of population, may be discerned in a single quotation.   Defoe, in his
" Tour," * published in 1727, speaks of Manchester as " one
of the greatest, if not really the greatest, mere village in
England."   He further adds, "Here, as at Liverpool, and as

* Espinasse, " Lancashire Worthies," 296 p.

at Frome, in Somersetshire, the town is extending in a surprising manner. Abundance, not of new houses only, but of
new streets of houses, are added, as also a new church,
dedicated to St. Anne, and they talk of another, and a fine
new square, so that the town is almost double to what it was
some years ago." The new church referred to we may presume
to be St. Mary's, but it was not consecrated until nearly forty
years after this. This delay, as we shall have occasion to show
hereafter, was the result of the protracted conflict between the
woollen and cotton manufacturers, the several legislative acts
which were passed in favour of the former having much
retarded the extension of the cotton industry, and as a consequence the growth of the town.

The description of Manchester at the beginning of the
eighteenth century, already quoted, was fitting. The town
ended on one side at Hunt's Bank, scaled the rising ground no
higher than Hanging Ditch, or, as it drew nearer Market-street
Lane, to what is now High-street. On the hither side of
this lane no church, therefore, was needed. Christ Church
answered all purposes here. The necessity for church accommodation arose in the neighbourhood of Deansgate on the one
side, and along the great London Road towards Piccadilly on
the other. At the bottom of Market-street Lane, marked in
those days by the Cross, was the juncture of several important
thoroughfares. Market-street Lane itself, as I have said, led
into the metropolitan road, Deansgate led into the Chester and
Liverpool roads. The shallow-bottomed vessels that bore raw
goods from Liverpool by the Mersey and the Irwell were unladed
close to the present Blackfriars Bridge. From the Market Place
the manufacturer, clad in his own fustian, doled out the raw
material, to receive it back from the weaver in woven cloth.
From the Market Place came or went the pack horsemen, with
tingling bell, to sell their goods as best they might, wherever
and whenever they might meet with a buyer. Here it was the

occasional coach started for, or set down its living freightage from, London, or Chester, or Hull, or Liverpool. The Market Place was marked out from the first as the bull's eye of Manchester. From the position of these several roads, however, it was manifest that any increase of population must be on the southern side of the town. It was so. By degrees, the number of householders increased in the neighbourhood of the Market Place, south and south-westwards. New tenements, too, were observable up Market-street Lane. It was seen, and required no prophetic eye to discern, that this increase must go on, and very soon the inhabitants began to talk idly, and ecclesiastic authorities more seriously, of the need of a new church.

In the Statutes at Large (anno 7 Annæ) will be found in the private legislation the following :—" An Act for building a church in the town of Manchester, in the county of Lancaster." This was in 1708. Four years after this, on the 12th July, a church was consecrated by Sir William Dawes, then Bishop of Chester, dedicated to Saint Ann. In this title were commemorated the virtues of the reigning queen, and the beneficence of Dame Ann Bland, lady of the manor of Manchester.

The new edifice was erected in Acres Field—a piece of corn-growing land some six and a half acres in extent—a portion sixty yards by forty having been surrendered from the south end for that purpose by William Baguley, gentleman, to whom it was seized.* The preamble to the Bill

* William Baguley, of Kearsley, was executor, and, as Canon Raines suggests, probably nephew of William Hulme, the noble founder of various local charities, notably the exhibitions connected with Brasenose College, Oxford. Mr. Baguley seems to have succeeded to his kinsman's spirit, for he, by will dated April 14, 1725, proved at Chester, gave £200 towards founding and endowing a charity school in Manchester. As above stated, he gave the site for the church. In addition to this he left £2 per annum for repairs out of lands in Deansgate. This money—the property having changed hands—is now paid by the Bartons of Stapleton Hall, Yorkshire, formerly of Swinton. As Manchester merchants they were closely connected with St. Ann's.

for building the church is somewhat long (vide Appendix to ch. 1), but out of it some interesting facts may be gleaned.

(1) It is stated to be erected with the approbation of the Queen, who is to be patroness in right of the Duchy of Lancaster. (Hence the dedication.) It is erected by subscription, and at the instance of certain inhabitants of the town. The advowson is to be in the hands of the Bishop of Chester. William Baguley allows 60 by 40 yards, situated about the middle of the south side of the close, to be cut off for the church-yard. Lady Bland and her successors in the manorial rights, one of which is the annual holding of a fair in the close, is content to curtail it. A wall is at once to be set up, enclosing the said allotment.

(2) The second paragraph appoints the Bishop of Chester and his successors to be actual patrons, the incumbent to bear the title of Rector of St. Ann's Church in Manchester, and to have freehold right of the place.

(3) The Rector is to be the recipient of money from all pews and seats, with consent of six or more inhabitants of the parish, to be from time to time commissioned by the Bishop for time being, whose actions are not to interfere with certain rights and dues attaching to the Warden and Fellows of the Collegiate Church. All fees and perquisites for Wardens, Fellows, Chaplain, Clerk, and Sextons, are to be theirs for weddings, christenings, churchings, and burials.

(4) There are no graves to be made in the body of the church—only in the yard. All burials, christenings, and weddings are to be registered at the Collegiate Church.

(5) The appointment of one or more Churchwardens is to be in the hand of the Bishop, so that the sacraments may be properly administered, and the ornaments be

preserved. These Wardens may take and purchase to themselves lands, tenements, etc., not to exceed the value of £50 per annum, for the provision of bread and wine, for repairs and beautifying the church, for utensils and ornaments, and to keep the same clean and secure.

(6) Acres Fair, if not finally extinguished, is to be curtailed in extent and manner of approach from Market Place and Deansgate.

(7) William Baguley, and heirs, and assignees, may " erect messuages, or buildings, or enclose gardens, courts, yards, and backsides in and out of the said close," always excepting the ground allotted to the new church and yard, and ways and streets leading to it.

(8) The eighth paragraph is long, but interesting. It contains directions relating to the new streets and square. The square is described as " a way to be left on the north side of the close called the Acres, straight and directly up to the said churchyard, of thirty yards broad." Then follow the side streets, leading from Cross-street to Deansgate, etc.

(9) These several ways are to be free and open to all as common highways. Also the private way into the close from Deansgate, belonging to William Baguley (now St. Ann's-street), is to be public after the consecration for coaches, carts, carriages, and for horses and cattle, and for the fair, if it be continued in a curtailed fashion.

(10) The lords of the manor of Manchester may still hold the fair at the usual time, subject to the new conditions of the place. If any new fairs be instituted, the tolls and dues are still to go to the owner of the manor.

The history of the fair, whose curtailment and possible

extinction is so carefully mentioned in this preamble, will be interesting to the general reader. It is a history of the Square. Robert Gresly, Baron of Manchester, who lived on the site of the present Chetham Hospital, gave tenure "to Aca, the clerk, of one (oxgang of) land of his lordship of Mamecestre for 3s. (yearly)." This, there need be little doubt, was Acres Field, or "Aca's Field," so called after the clerk.* In 1222, this same Robert obtained a temporary permission to hold a fair in Manchester. The grant is dated Lewknor, August 11, 1222. The baron is to give the king, then in his minority, a palfrey by way of acknowledgment. In 1227 Henry III. came of age, and the grant was renewed for ever. Manchester Corporations and the year 1876 were not thought of. The fair was to be held during three days, the eve, the day, and the morrow of St. Matthew. It is to be conducted well and quietly, and not to be injurious to neighbouring fairs. This final grant was dated from Farringdon, 15th August, 1227. (Baines, i. 274.) The fair thus held was conducted annually till the time of the erection of St. Ann's Church. As already noted, the Act of 1708 provided for the partial extinction of the fair. It was foreseen that the ground would henceforth be too confined for its cus-

---

* It is but fair to add that "Acres," or "the Acres," was a common locative term in early days. At first acre had no reference to a statute measure, and denoted simply a plowed field (Latin *ager*). In ninetenths of our local compounds, of which it is an ingredient, the original sense is implied. Thus, such surnames as "Goodacre," "Longacre," "Oddiker" (oat-acre), or "Whittaker" (wheat-acre), have arisen. The old name for a plowman was *acreman*, or *akerman*. Hence the surnames "Aikerman," "Acreman," "Acherman," and the corrupted "Aikman." Thus Acres Field may have been originally but the "plowed field." I cannot forbear noticing that in "God's acre," *i.e.*, the churchyard, all the beauty of the word lies in the primary meaning. The burial yard is "God's acre," that is, "God's ploughed field," where the seed sown by Him in corruption shall be reaped an incorruptible body. It is curious to note that a family of the name of "Acres" lived in Manchester up to the beginning of the present century.

tomary wants. The church took a large slice from the south end of the close, and power was given to build around it and upon certain portions of it. Originally the field comprised some six and a half acres. More than half of this was wanted. Nevertheless, the fair went on. Two days were occupied in its conduct in the stead of three. Toll Lane was kept open for the passage of cattle ; and till within a generation Toll Lane retained the name to remind us how the Cheshire farmer obtained ingress for himself, his cattle, and country produce. The toll went to the lord of the manor. A great change occurred in 1823. St. Ann's Square had become too crowded a thoroughfare for fairs. It was removed at first, I believe, to Campfield, in Deansgate. For the past six hundred years had Manchester seen an annual fair on the site of Acres Field. After all, the old order changeth but slowly. It is worth while to add that, during the remainder of the year, the Acres Close was used for farming purposes. Mr. Harland has given us the reminiscences of certain old men and women who lived about 1780. All could remember corn or potatoes growing in the present square.* The crop was reaped in the autumn, and as St. Matthew's Day fell on September 21, everything was in readiness for the fair. How strangely all sounds in the light of the present condition of the town. It is on this very plot that Cobden's statue stands. I leave the political economist to draw the parallel. There are not a few men who could weave a connected story out of the private institution and public abolition of this fair, and the principles, the aims, and the triumphs of the great apostle of free trade. To them I leave the task.

* Benjamin Oldham, aged 83 (in 1787), could remember corn and potatoes growing in St. Ann's Square, which were obliged to be carted away the day before the fair, as the people had a right to come to hold the fair, whether removed or not. This same Oldham could recollect carrots and turnips growing on the plot where the then Exchange stood.—Manchester Collect. ii. 188.

Defoe, writing in 1727, speaks of the Square as yet in prospective. But it could not have been far from completion, for in the following year (July 24) Byrom writes in his diary, " Mrs. Byrom gone to Mr. Brooks's in the Square, and nobody but myself at home." Mr. Baguley, therefore, must have early begun to build upon and about the enclosure.

There were at this time in Manchester two branches of the Mosley family—one living at Ancoats Hall, and the other at Hulme Hall. To go to either from the Market Place was to pass through lanes skirted by green fields shaded by trees. Ancoats was as distinct from Manchester proper then as Islington from London when John Gilpin made his famous journey. Nicholas Mosley dwelt at Ancoats ; the ancestor of the present Sir Thomas Mosley. Edward lived at Hulme. He was an ardent lover of liberty, and beheld with satisfaction the Revolution of 1688, which seated William the Third on the throne of this country. Evidently his sense of satisfaction was known to that monarch, for a year afterwards he was made Sir Edward Mosley, at Whitehall, although he was 72 years old. His wife was Jane Meriel, daughter of Richard Saltonstall, of Huntwick, near Halifax. She had been most strictly trained in the principles of the Presbyterians, and died in 1695, two years after her husband, in loyal adherence to her sect. She left £50 to the poor of that denomination. She helped to build the chapel in Pool Fold (Cross-street Chapel) for Mr. Newcome ; and when his funeral sermon was preached therein in 1695, the year of her own death, Mr. Chorlton dedicated the published discourse to her.

Anne Mosley, their sole child and heiress—two boys had died—married Sir John Bland, of Kippax Park, Yorkshire. The Bland family came from Bland's Gill, in the North Riding. Sir Thomas Bland, Knight, settled at Kippax in the reign of Elizabeth, or perhaps a few years after her death. His grandson, Sir Thomas Bland, was made first baronet in 1642 ; his son, Sir John Bland, being the suitor for Anne Mosley. They were married in 1685, the bridegroom not being yet of legal age. His vices had evidently been carefully concealed alike from the bride's parents and herself. His affection, if any had been inspired, soon failed, and practically deserting her he rushed into every dissipation that his wife's money could purchase for him. At the gaming table he soon bid fair to ruin himself and her. Having sat twice in Parliament—once for Appleby, and again for Pontefract, near which town Kippax lies—he died in 1715, regretted, probably, by none, save those who had won his money, and who, perchance, hoped to win more. This was not Lady Bland's only trouble. Her only surviving son, John, seemed bent on following closely in his father's steps. The gaming table quickly reduced his patrimony—it had been a splendid one—and to pay his evil debts the whole of his mother's estate, so far as was possible, had to be sold. By his own and the death of his two sons the baronetcy became extinct in 1756.

Lady Bland, widowed of father, mother, and husband, resided altogether at Hulme Hall. She was undoubtedly popular in Manchester, even among the High Church faction : very affable, very amiable, and evidently strongly religious. As a set off to these virtues, she was self-willed, passionate, and somewhat Elizabethan. The fashions of the town flowed from her.* From father and mother she had inherited Low Church (to use the new term) if not Presbyterian tendencies ; and when Henry Newcome, the Presbyterian minister, the friend of the family,

---

* Lady Bland had her public days as well as private, when she endeavoured, in her coach and four, to outshine Lady Drake, the leader of the High Church fashionables. A leader of Low Church fashion in the newly-erected Assembly Room, she is said to have been on one occasion so annoyed with the brilliant display of Stuart tartan by the High Church ladies that she led her party in orange ribbons into the street, and danced by moonlight.—Halley, ii. 285.

died, she was well prepared to become foundress of a new church, which, necessitated as it was by the increasing population, might also become a religious rendezvous for the Hanoverian party in the town.

The foundation stone of the church was laid May 18th, 1709, by Lady Bland. Her subscription towards the erection had been a bountiful one. Her interest in the undertaking was at once personal and political. It was fitting this honour should be hers. Over three years was occupied in completing the building. It was not till July, 1712, that the edifice was ready for consecration. On the west door is inscribed the following:—" Ecclesiæ hujus sola benefactorum munificentia extructæ fundimenta facta die, xviii. Maii, A.D. mdccix. Totum opus absolutum et consecratum die xvii. Julii, A.D. mdccxii."

Mr. Byrom, commonly called Dr. John Byrom, writing to his brother, July 9th, 1712, says in a postscript, " Do you know that the new church is to be consecrated on the 17th instant?" The day of consecration seems to have been a great holiday to the townsfolk : all work was stayed, all the houses were empty. Everybody was pushing his way to the plot of ground that was still partly but a field, some to see the solemn rite performed, some to see the grandees arrive. The Mosleys, of Ancoats, and the Blands, from Hulme Hall, in their yellow coaches, Sir William Dawes, the bishop, who died Archbishop of York, Mr. Baguley, and the representative families of the town, all were present. The church looked new and handsome, and the townspeople were very proud of it. No doubt it was considered a very noble pile in its day. It was built after the fashion of many London churches of that date, being Corinthian in style. For lack of a Manchester daily paper to fall back upon, we must be content with two extracts, one from a letter, another from a diary. Mr. Byrom—doubtless he was present on the occasion—writing from London to his wife thirteen years afterwards, says: "Mr. Hooper,* Clowes,† and I went in a coach, and light at Holborn, and went into St. Andrew's Church. It was the model, I believe, of the new church at Manchester." Edmund Harrold, a peruke maker, of whom we shall speak again, writes in his diary :—" 1712. July 17. Remarkable for St. Ann's Church consecration, and a great concourse of people. Good business, and I sober at eight o'clock at night, but I was merry before I went to bed. Bishop Dawes performed the consecration, Mr. Baguley endowed it, the clergy responded at entrance. Mr. Ainscough read prayers. Beatman 'sponsed (acted as clerk). The bishop read the gift both in Latin and English. Mr. Band (Mr. Bann, the appointed rector) preached on ' Holiness becometh Thine house, O Lord,' then the bishop, and clergy, and who would, stayed sacrament. Thus they were about four hours in this great work." The communion table, with rich velvet cover, was a special gift of Lady Bland.

To us who live in an age of so much religious zeal, the consecration of a single church may seem but a trifling matter. It was otherwise then. An appalling deadness had come over English Christianity with the restoration of Charles II. As a reaction from the religious hypocrisy of the Common-

* Francis Hooper was librarian at the Hospital after the death of Mr. Leicester. At this time he was minister of Didsbury Chapel.

† This was Joseph Clowes, father of the first rector of S. John's. "Clowes" is a good old local name, and by its dress proves itself to be of North English origin. It is but another form of "Clough." "Enough" and "enow" are a parallel illustration, for both directory and dictionary are formed from the same materials. "Hough" and "How," as local surnames, are but another case in point. A *clough* is a narrow ravine.

"These caitif Jewes did not so now
Send him to seeke in clif and clow."
Cursor Mundi.

The terminative "s" is common, as in "Styles," "Mills," "Milnes," etc. The name is often written "Cloughs" in old registers.

wealth, it was natural, in a sense inevitable ; none the less was it lamentable. The latter part of the seventeenth century saw scarce a stride made by the Church to overtake a fast-increasing population. Our activity in the building of churches only truly dates from the commencement of the eighteenth century. Birmingham began the good work, Liverpool followed, and Manchester brought up the rear.

Mr. Prescott informed Bishop Gastrell (Chester), in 1717, that only nine churches, large and small, had been consecrated in the diocese since the Restoration, a period of nearly sixty years. Of these, two were in Liverpool and one in Manchester. (Not. Cest. ii. 77.) In this report it is added of St. Ann's :— " It is worth about £100 per annum arising from the pews, which are to be let by the minister with the consent of six or more of the inhabitants commissioned by the Bishop for any number of years not exceeding twenty-one."—" There are two Churchwardens appointed by the Bishop according to Act of Parliament, who are made a corporation to receive benefactions not exceeding £50 per annum for the repairs and utensils of the church, and providing bread and wine for ye sacrament."

A statement is also added of charities connected with the same church :—"Given to this church an: 1717, by Mr. (George) Grimshaw £1,000 to be laid out (by his executors, Mr. William Hunter and Mr. John Diggles, both of Manchester) in a rent charge, or estate of fee simple for (the) rector, (the) interest in meantime to be paid to the rector."

" Given for repairing this church by William Baguley, gent., £2 per annum out of lands in Deansgate."

Also " by Mr. Samuel Heywood, £4. 16s. per annum out of lands in Sholver " (Oldham).*

* St. Ann's may boast of having some of the most massive silver communion plate in the north of England. The service has been put together at different periods, and comprises eighteen pieces, A large alms dish and two flagons are each inscribed as follows :—"Given to St. Ann's Church by

Frank Smedley—how impossible to Mister or Esquire him—
that most genial writer of healthful stories, speaks in one of
his books—Lewis Arundel, I think—of Manchester Collegiate
Church as "th' owd church." How familiarly the term falls
upon the ear of a denizen of this great industrial centre. To
the poor the sacred pile goes by no other name. Let others
call it Christ Church, and others the Collegiate Church, and
others the Cathedral. These sobriquets, some old, some young,
are not a tithe as venerable to them as "th' owd church." In
"th' owd church" they were baptised ; there they were joined
in wedlock ; there, in death, until its yard was full, they were
carried forth to burial. 'Tis true in too many cases baptism
was but a form, and wedlock far from being looked upon as
holy ; but none the less over "th' owd church" hangs a halo
of sacred association which in their worst moments they cannot
forget. The pedigree of the populace and the country round
lies in the tablets and registers of "th' owd church." And yet
this term, around which cluster so many memories, is after all
but a new name. That is, it is but one hundred and sixty
years old—no ancient title for a church. "Th' owd church,"
as such, was unknown until the new church of St. Ann arose,
from which it was to be contra-distinguished. It may seem

Mr. Edward Mosley, son of Oswald Mosley, Esq., of Ancoats, in ye parish
of Manchester, 1714." Two patens, two chalices, and one large flagon are
the gift of John Sandiford, each bearing the title, " Ex dono Johannis
Sandiford." On these there is no date, but the hall-marks betoken the
year 1712, which proves them to have been given upon the consecration of
the church. Mr. Sandiford lived in the Millgate. (Pole Booke, p. 33.)
Two small patens are without inscription, but are of the same date. One
circular and most massive alms dish bears the simple inscription, "St.
Ann's Church, Manchester." The hall-mark is 1712. Whether bought
by subscription or the gift of some individual donor, I cannot say. In 1838
John Ollivant, Esq., of the firm of Ollivant and Botsford, gave the church
two silver cups, which gift incited some member or members of the congregation to provide two others in 1841.

strange, but in the minds of the poorer classes St. Ann's got
her name only to be forgotten.   She is never St. Ann's,
but always "th' new church."   As such the Collegiate Church
became "th' owd church."   A new inn in Hanging Ditch was
started.   Its swinging sign displayed in gorgeous colouring a
picture of the edifice that had been erected in Acres Field.   As
a matter of course it was called the "New Church Inn."

Dr. Byrom, writing August 19, 1725, says: "Thursday.   Mr.
Cattell and I went to the top of the *old* church steeple.   At
the *new* church at night."*   Again, on June 13, 1733, he writes:
"J. Brook preached at the *new* church to-day, morning and
evening.   I was at the *old* church morning, *new* afternoon."
Edmund Harrold, in his diary, speaks for a few weeks of St.
Ann's and Christ Church.   Three days after the consecration,
he says: "Great work at St. Ann's, but I was at Christ
Church."   Very speedily, however, these titles are dropped,
and it is "the new church" and "the old church" with him.
Until the consecration of St. Mary's, in 1756, these two names
were in the common mouth, and had these two churches remained alone until to-day, St. Ann's would have still been "the
new church."   But with the erection of the third sanctuary, the
second was compelled to fall back upon its ecclesiastical title.
This in no way affected "th' owd church."   The name lived
on, and will live so long as the edifice stands.†

Morning and afternoon prayers were read at both churches,
and it was the popular custom to attend both places of worship.   If Dr. Byrom is seen at the Collegiate Church in the
morning, hearkening to one of the fellows, he will be found
in the after part of the day not far from Lady Bland's pew,

---

* The day before this he writes : "Played at piquet with Dr. Malyn
and Mr. Guy : beat them, won five groats : thence to the new church."—
Byrom's Remains, vol. 1, 176.

† The *Graphic* (October 14th, 1876) states that it was called the "old
church" in the times of the civil wars of Charles the First.   This is a
mistake.

listening to Mr. Bann. He knows an invitation to tea is possible. Mr. Joseph Clowes, father of the first rector of St. John's, must needs attend both churches on the Sunday, and if Edmund Harrold can occasionally write that he has been at "th' new church both ends," it is only because the Jacobitism of the Collegiate Church has driven him more completely to the Hanoverian sanctuary in Acres Field.

There have been ten rectors of St. Ann's during a period of 164 years. The average duration of each incumbency has been over sixteen years.

> Nathaniel Bann . . . . . 1712—1736.
> Joseph Hoole . . . . . 1736—1745.
> Abel Ward . . . . . . 1745—1785.
> Rowland Sandford . . . . 1785—1795.*
> Robert Barker . . . . . 1795—1822.†
> Henry Law . . . . . . 1822—1825.‡
> Jeremiah Smith . . . . . 1825—1837.§
> Henry Walter Mc.Grath . . 1837—1852.
> John Richardson . . . . 1852—1857.
> James Bardsley . . . . . 1857—

* The *Manchester Mercury*, Tuesday, January 7, 1795, says: "Wednesday evening, at Harrogate, the Rev. R. Sandford, rector of St. Ann's Church. His examplary conduct in his profession, his benevolent attention to his inferiors, and his warm, unaffected attachment to those who had the pleasure of his society will be long remembered, and his death sincerely regretted." He was buried at St. Ann's. His widow lived to an advanced age in John-street; and it was a familiar sight to see her carried in her chair to daily prayers at St. Ann's. She was one of the lady visitors to the Sunday-schools for many years. She died October 30, 1817.

† Robert Barker held the vicarage of Astley with the rectorship of St. Ann's. There is scarcely a trace of his presence in the registers of the Manchester Church. The work was carried on by an indefatigable curate, Matthew Randall by name. Mr. Barker died and was buried at Astley, in 1822. It is possible he was a former curate of St. Ann's, for we find that a daughter of his was baptised there, August 29, 1769.

C

Of these ten rectors four are still living, viz., Henry Law, Dean of Gloucester ; Canon Mc.Grath, John Richardson, and Canon Bardsley. Of the six who are dead, three lie in St. Ann's churchyard. It is my purpose to give a brief account of the life and labours of but three. The first two lived in times of trouble. The third saw those troubles terminate. To speak of them is to speak of the political history of their day. I can touch upon these things but shortly. Conflictive claims to the English throne we trust are matters of the past.

The church, unlike the parish, has undergone but little change, save that which attaches to growing years. Smoke and grime have done their full share in adding an appearance of wrinkled age to the fabric. Much of the stonework is crumbling into decay; nevertheless, the exterior of the church is as it was in everything but the tower. Originally, as the old woodcuts show, there was a cupola, but in 1777 this was

‡ Henry Law, the present Dean of Gloucester, vacated the living of St. Ann's over 50 years ago. He is son of George Henry Law (who was promoted to the see of Chester in 1812) and therefore nephew of the great Lord Ellenborough. His grandfather was Edmund Law, Bishop of Carlisle, born at Cartmel, in 1703. His great-grandfather was rector of Cartmel, in Lancashire. It is not often that there are four successive generations of clergymen, or that two of them should be bishops, and the third a dean. The family, as the name denotes, are of North English extraction. Dean Law is best known as the author of " Christ is All," a series of books explaining the Christology of the Pentateuch. They have reached a circulation of over 100,000, and are notable for their exquisite simplicity.

§ Dr. Smith needs no mention. He succeeded Mr. Lawson as head master of the Grammar School in 1807, and held the post 30 years. Part of this time he was curate of St. Mark's, Cheetham Hill. In 1813 he became incumbent of St. Peter's, and in 1825 rector of St. Ann's. Resigning the mastership and rectorship in 1837, he retired to Great Wilbraham, near Cambridge (presented to him in 1832). He died in 1854, aged 84. A full account of him will be found in his son's " Register of the Manchester Grammar School."

removed, as it appeared to be in danger of falling. Owing to several accidents in other parts of the town, there had sprung up a general panic on the subject. A subscription having been raised, to which Sir John Parker Mosley added largely, thus keeping up the traditional connection of his family with the church, a steeple replaced the tottering cupola. But this arrangement was far from satisfying the occupants of houses in the immediate neighbourhood. To them it was but a new peril. Backed by the inhabitants of the Square and King-street, they raised their voices against the new spire, and successfully, for after standing but a few years, this also was removed. A few yards of solid masonry were then raised upon the original tower, and it became as it now is.

An alteration of a different character took place in 1817. Until that time the method of entry from King-street to the Square was through the churchyard of St. Ann's. The houses abutted upon the yard, the doors lying to what would now be called the back of the premises. The belated urchin attending church on Sunday, or desirous of speedy egress into the Square on the week-day, had but to drop from the parlour window into the yard, and make his way through the gate. A pathway exterior to the wall led away from the Arcade into Cross-street. This was called St. Ann's Alley, or St. Ann's Lane. The rest was entirely occupied by the graveyard.

Chiefly by the aid of the late Canon Parkinson, Vicar-General to Bishop Law, and the churchwardens, Henry Cardwell and William Heslop, this state of things was altered. The gravestones were crumbling, and the epitaphs were fast becoming obliterated by the tread of constant feet. The state of the yard had become a scandal. With the bishop's consent rails were erected at an average distance of six feet from the adjacent walls. The graves exterior to this boundary were covered with soil, and flagged above; and henceforward the foot passenger had a way for himself.*   This speedily caused doors to be set on the new pathway. In time, shops took the place of dwelling-houses; and now this little road is one of the most thronged of Manchester thoroughfares from early morning till set of day.

One other change may be mentioned. When Canon Mc.Grath came to the church in 1837, it was found to be in a deplorable condition. There had been no real attempt at repairs for a hundred and twenty-five years. Mr. Percival, an attendant in Dr. Smith's time, and first clerk to Mr. Mc.Grath, tells me that the windows were literally blocked up with accumulation of dust, and the entire fabric was "neither wind nor water tight." At a cost of £2,000 the whole was renovated. I believe it was then the large, square pillars were rounded. A gentleman said that he had "heard Mr. Mc.Grath preach for two years, but now for the first time he had seen him." The late Archbishop Sumner, then Bishop of Chester, preached the reopening sermon to a crowded congregation. So improved was the appearance of the church, outside and inside, that it was looked upon as a re-consecration.

If, however, the church of St. Ann has altered but little, it cannot so be said of the parish. We have already defined its limits. Of course, they are more circumscribed than they have been. Beginning with a rambling population that struck out Market-street way on one hand and Deansgate way on the other, the time came when the interstices began to be filled up. As the boundaries of the town widened, the work became too great for one clergyman. Other churches, like St. James's, St. Mary's, St. John's, and St. Peter's, took share in it, and eventually, Mosley-street, Market-street, Deansgate, Brasenose-street, and Princess-street, became the legal limits

* The last burial in St. Ann's yard took place May 31, 1854—that of Richard Smith, of Hanover-street, aged 16. The Rev. George Philpot, then curate of St. Ann's, and now rector of Gorton, conducted the service.

of the parish. During the course of 160 years, a population has settled and fled from the place. But the old residents have left their memorial. Putting aside the names that commemorate royal personages, the titles of our central streets are well nigh all but the cenotaphs of merchantmen who once dwelt in the lanes and by-roads to which they have bequeathed their names. So comparatively recent is the growth of our street nomenclature, that there is little or no difficulty in tracing its origin. Here we have a distinct advantage over London. We are not in risk of explaining Billiter Lane, like the great London historian, as the street in which men who were occupied in the trade of "billet" making (*i.e.*, preparation of firewood) dwelt. The billiter was the old "bell-founder," but two hundred years ago the term had become sufficiently obsolete to be unknown to Stowe, so quickly do words spring up, flourish, and die. It is, indeed, an easier task with us in Manchester, for all is modern. In 1650 there were not more than twenty-four streets and lanes in the village that has developed into a city. One hundred years later, according to Berry's plan, there were one hundred and fifty, and the good old grocer remarks in a note that the population had doubled within thirty years. "A new parish has been erected," he says, not in the happiest of English, "and a large sumptuous church built thereon, called St. Ann's, also several streets, squares (he is including the new squares of St. James, and Mr. Marsden), are new built, and many of the new houses are elegant and magnificent structures," all of which was strictly true, for Manchester men were growing opulent, and wealth breeds luxury.

I cannot forbear dwelling upon these streets that bound and interlace the parish of St. Ann. They are known by names that, meaningless as they may seem to some, are full of gossip of the past. Silent those street signs may be, but only as books are silent. Unclasp them, and they are rare reading. These busy thoroughfares were not so long ago but lanes that led through meadows or by garden walls to the more elegant abode of some notable merchant.

Brown-street was originally Brown's-street—that is, the street where Mr. Brown lived. It would be a popular affix. We do not know who Mr. Brown was, but we can prove that Mr. Cooper dwelt at the end of Cooper's-street—not Cooper-street then—in 1751, and Joshua Marriott, a great St. Annite, in Marriott's Court, and Mr. Marsden in Marsden's Square. These two latter gentlemen lived in very substantial houses of the old formal style, squarely fronted, balustraded above, with the customary shallow flight of steps leading into the street, The spring that gave water to Manchester for generations, and sufficed for all, was sponsor for "Spring Gardens" and "Fountain-street," and tells of sweet ruralities that are conspicuous by their absence. By means of pipes its waters were brought to the conduit in the Market Place, and thus the inhabitants who dwelt by the cross were saved the necessity of climbing the ascent. Tib Lane reminds us that one of our smaller rivulets flows, or did flow, secretly beneath the palatial warehouses of that neighbourhood. Mulberry-street acquired its title from the great mulberry tree close to Mr. Nicholl's residence, and fast by the site of the present Roman Catholic church. Cross-street reminds us that the cross no longer adorns the Market Place ; while in the name of Pool Fold we can still picture the murky ditch of St. Plungeon's, with its ducking stool for scolds. The casual stroller in Chapel Walks, wandering thither of an evening with his pipe, would be an amused spectator of the scene, no doubt. Hyde Park*— stare not, good reader, the rectors of St. Ann's knew the spot well—was the little space now consecrated by the presence of the Thatched House Tavern. The origin of the name is obvious! The spot was composed of but a few square yards; no tree could grow there, no member of royalty

* Hyde Park disappeared in 1786, having to make way for the meat market built by Mr. Chadwick. This was also removed in 1803.

had even been seen there, and even a single horseman would have found it difficult to turn his steed in it! Pall Mall has fared better, though its proportions are not magnificent. Brasenose-street and Hulme-street remain as a memorial of Hulme, and his bequest to the Oxford College. Ridgefield, once "Ridge-Field," and at first "Ridge's Field," still survives the changes of time; but the field is gone, as are the Ridges who dwelt there.* Some few names have altogether disappeared. All that piece of rising ground from Deansgate up Queen-street and Back Queen-street was "The Mount." Mount-street alone remains to record the fact. The windmill that surmounted this elevation gave its name to Windmill-street, and existed till 1811.† Toll Lane, too, is gone, though it is but a generation since it became obsolete. I have already recounted its origin. In Barton Arcade is commemorated a family who for generations have been baptised, married, and buried at St. Ann's.

If street nomenclature goes for anything, then St. Ann's is the most loyal parish in England. There were originally three Queen-streets existing within or bordering upon its legal limits. Only one remains. St. Ann-street was at first Queen-street. Then by way of distinction it was styled "Queen-street, St. Ann's." Finally it received its present title. A second Queen-street was and is that wherein St. Ann's Schools are situated. The third was what we now term Upper King-street. The fact is this part was never intended to be a street at all, but a private square, to vie in its substantial grandeur with St. Ann's Square. It was called St. James's Square, but it was lengthened, the conception was spoilt, and after some years, St. James was content to

---

* The Directory of 1772 has "Miss Ridge, boarding school in Back Square" (Red Lyon Square). This is the last record of the Ridges I can find. Imagine a young ladies' boarding-house in Back Square.

† Mr. Procter, in his valuable "Memorials," quotes an advertisement from the *Manchester Mercury* of 1766, offering "the windmill at the top of Deansgate" for sale—Deansgate then reaching no further than Peter-street.

migrate into his present obscurity lower down. The Hanoverian queen again asserted her prerogative against the claims
of a Jacobite Pretender.* In process of time, other royal
titles found favour. The parish can still boast a King-street,
commemorative of one of the Georges, a Lower King-street, a
Princess-street, a Clarence-street, a York-street (Cumberland-
street is just outside), and an Albert Square, while the pedestrian
as he quits the earlier square dedicated to Queen Anne, enters
upon Victoria-street. All these titles are memorials of royal
personages who have lived since the accession of the Hanoverian queen ; it is very manifest, therefore, that although St.
Ann's parish lies in the heart of the town, it is of modern
origin. How youthful must be the suburbs !

The character of St. Ann's Square is fast changing. Buildings
of modern style have superseded the original houses, where opulent and substantial merchants dwelt. The trees, once so carefully preserved by wooden framework, and planted at equal dis-
tances, no longer line the curbstone,† to remind the spectator
that our forefathers intended the place to be but a copy of the
fashionable squares of Bath or London. Private residences
have given way to public establishments. Acres Court, with its

---

* The original St. James's Square was built at the very period when the
Jacobites and Nonjurors were at greatest feud with the Whig portion of the
townspeople. As this was the spot where most of the collegiate clergy
lived, there can be little doubt that the title was given in opposition to the
Hanoverian square lower down. It is one more memorial of a conflict
which is now but a matter of history.

† Mr. Procter "marvels how such trees withstood the wind and storm
that swept the county in 1703, or braved the hurricane of 1802, when one
of the dial-plates of St. Ann's clock was forced from its position." (Manchester Streets, page 258.) Usually so accurate, the author is at fault here.
These trees were not planted till the square was laid out some fifteen years
after the storm of 1703, and I am not sure that they were standing in 1802.
I rather imagine that the public will, which oftentimes beats with more force
than any tempestuous gale, had already swept them away.

"Dark Entry" and more perilous avenue for traffic, has disappeared; and now, after further alteration, Exchange-street reigns more nobly in its stead. Ravald's coffee-house, over the court, where gossips frequented, is an institution of the past; Parker's and Bancroft's supply the deficiency. And yet St. Ann's Square remains the same in one respect. It is the lounging place of Manchester—the haunt of the young spark, who is sometimes a coxcomb—the scene of feminine triumphs in dress—the chosen spot for accidental rencontres. It was all this just a hundred years ago. The peruke and ribbon is wanting to the staider citizen, and the rapier to the exquisite, but only the dress is different. The little world of St. Ann's Square is wagging as it did when our great grandmothers were in their teens, and arranging their furbelows wherewith to dazzle our great-grandfathers under the trees of the Square, or by Newton's shop, that stood by Whipp's, the saddler. Fashion so fickle in dress is in Manchester, at least, faithful to the scene of its exhibition.

II.

NATHANIEL BANN,
1712-1736.

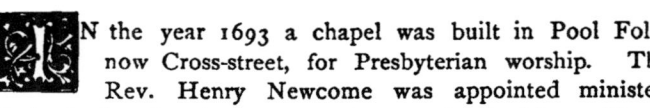

N the year 1693 a chapel was built in Pool Fold, now Cross-street, for Presbyterian worship. The Rev. Henry Newcome was appointed minister. Indeed, the chapel was erected expressly for him. Henry Newcome came to Manchester in 1656 to succeed Richard Hollingworth at the Collegiate Church. He was never elected fellow, but, as stipendiary curate, crowded the walls of that edifice to overflowing by his simple and earnest discourses. In 1662 the Act of Uniformity was passed, and Newcome vacated his post. He preached his last sermon in an ecclesiastic pulpit in Bowdon Church, while staying with his staunch Presbyterian friend Lord Delamere, at Dunham Park.

Henry Newcome had many sympathisers in the town. One of his closest and most familiar associates was Dr. Nathaniel Bann, the leading physician of the place, having a house in Market-street Lane, and, as we gather from Newcome's diary, Lady Bland's professional attendant. Dr. Bann and Mr. Newcome are frequently found together at Hulme Hall and in the neighbourhood of Dunham. It is interesting to note that

Nathaniel Bann, the first rector of St. Ann's, was the son of the most intimate lay friend of Henry Newcome, himself first minister of the closely-situated chapel in Pool Fold. This connection was not accidental, as will be easily seen. The Mosleys had sympathised with the Presbyterian curate. Lady Meriel, the wife of Sir Edward Mosley, had been up to the time of her death his great patroness. She had helped him in his pecuniary difficulties, for when scruples of conscience urged him to vacate his post he had a large family dependent upon him, and no immediate hopes of obtaining a livelihood. Lady Mosley's daughter Ann, afterwards Lady Bland, was equally attached to him. He had been her mother's friend and spiritual adviser ; he became her own. When his chapel in Cross-street (to use the modern name) was erected, Mosleys were found to be among the first to sit under his short-lived ministry therein.

With Newcome's death Lady Bland's interest in the chapel seems to have terminated. She was herself a thorough Church-woman, but belonged to that section which only a few years after took or received the name of the Low Church party. It is quite possible that if Newcome had lived St. Ann's would not have been built. Certainly its erection would have been delayed, for without the large offerings of several of the minister's friends, it would have been found impossible to entertain the project of establishing a new church. But Henry Newcome died, and St. Ann's was built. The first appointment lay practically in the hands of the foundress. Nothing could be more natural than that she should present to the living one upon whose head in his childhood Henry Newcome's hand must oft have been set while he breathed a blessing upon the young Nathaniel. Nathaniel Bann was the son of Lady Meriel's medical attendant—the son, too, of one of Newcome's closest associates. It was but harmonising certain conflicting interests of a religious and social character to prefer young Bann to the rectorship of the new church.

I strongly suspect that the Banns had been established in Manchester for several generations. It is quite possible, and fairly probable, that Captain Band, injured in the skirmish that took place when Lord Strange besieged Manchester, in 1642, was grandfather of the rector.* The difference of spelling need present no difficulty. Both Dr. Bann and his son are styled Band on several occasions. The young rector's baptismal record in the registers of the Collegiate Church runs thus :— " 1671. December 14. Nathaniel, son of Nathaniel Band, of Manchester, phisitian." Even Dr. Byrom, writing in 1725, says, " To-night, Mr. Band, Samuel, and Joseph Clowes, and I, were at Mr. Falconer's." The burial register of the rector, also at the Collegiate Church, is entered, "September 10th, 1736. Rev. Nathaniel Band, rector of St. Ann's, at St. Ann's." The fact is, the orthography of proper names, even among the most cultivated classes, was far from being settled for several generations after this. Another member of the Bann family resided in the Market Place, a Mrs. Mary Banne † being found in the " Pole Booke " at the close of the seventeenth century. This connection with the Parliamentary captain is all the more probable, inasmuch as Dr. Bann was a warm friend of the Manchester Presbyterians.

It is pleasant to think that the first rector must have spent the whole of his life, saving his college career, within a stone's throw or two of the place of his birth and the sphere of his ministry. In all probability, he was born in his own future parish. At an early age he would, as a matter of course, be sent to the Grammar School, and from there to the University. On saints' days he would attend Christ Church with his fellow-

---

* " Master Band was shot in the thigh. After they had ceased two or three houres they ended the battle with the sun of the day. Captain Band is well recovered again, praised be God."—Civil War Tracts : Lancashire, p. 26.

† Mrs. Mary Banne, Markett Place, £0. 1s. 0d. —P. 26.

scholars ; on Sundays he would accompany his father to listen
to the more private exhortations of Henry Newcome. Probably
it was while at the school in the Millgate that he learnt to love
the quiet seclusion of that room in the Chetham's Library,
which is perhaps unrivalled in the kingdom for the true *genius
loci*. That he was of a studious and meditative mood, his
everyday book, still sacredly preserved in that library, fully
testifies. Perchance, as he sat in that quaint oriel, with its
panes of mellowed colours, his highest dream was that some
future day he might wander amid those dim corridors as official
guardian of its treasures. * Be this so, his ambition was fulfilled.
At the age of twenty-two, and in the year 1693, he was
appointed librarian, upon the death of Thomas Pendleton.
This post he held till he became rector of St. Ann's. In
the meantime, however, he was ordained chaplain to Christ
Church. Of his life at this period little is known. In 1701,
his name occurs in the registers of Didsbury Chapel as
having taken duty there.† The close connection of the Blands
with that chapelry will make his presence there perfectly
natural. Little could Mr. Bann have thought, while he daily
attended upon his duties in the library, that a hundred and
fifty years after this the diary of Henry Newcome would
be among its printed treasures, and his own studied reflections among its manuscript curiosities. The visitor to that
noble library may, if he will, see a book knife, whereon is
inscribed the name of the custodian, afterwards rector of
St. Ann's.

About the appointment, as we have seen, there could be
little doubt. The times were serious, and growing more serious
every day. Lady Bland would not submit that a Jacobite
should occupy the pulpit of a church built out of Hanoverian

, * Dr. Bann, his father, had been elected feoffee of the Hospital in 1681. —
Adam Martindale, p. 209.

† Didsbury and Chorlton Chapelries, p. 92.

pockets. The warden of the Collegiate Church, the silver-tongued Wroe, was himself a Whig. The only objection would be the fellows. However much the new church might by them be considered a chapel of ease, it was a distinct parish, and they could not control the election. Therefore they would be pleased, doubtless, that the choice, such as it was, should fall upon one of themselves. And, indeed, if Mr. Clayton, a strict Jacobite and fellow, bore the same affection for Nathaniel Bann in his earlier as in his later days, he must himself have viewed the appointment with genuine pleasure. The new rector preached the consecration sermon, his text being, as Harrold informs us, Psalm xciii. 5, "Holiness becometh Thine house, O Lord." The Sunday following the church was crowded, morning and evening, by the townsfolk, many of whom had been unable to obtain admission on the Thursday. The church had been nearly four years building; and a new church, and especially such a handsome pile as this, was a great event, indeed, in those days. On the following Thursday the appropriation of pews by the chief subscribers was formally permitted. This objectionable practice was in its highest glory at this time, and its ill effects still bear fruit in different parts of the diocese. The names of several of these gentlemen still remain on the brass labels attached to the doors of their pews. Thus we find, "Robert Stott, July 24, 1712; Henry Townley, July 24, 1712; James Beck, July 24, 1712; Humfrey Oldfield, 1712." Many pew doors show indentures where brass plates have formerly rested. Doubtless, some of these must be referred to the same date. In other cases there will have been an exchange of labels. These four alone represent the pews appropriated by subscribers to the building fund.

Fortunately for those who are interested in the history of St. Ann's, we are not without information relative to the early life of the young church. Edmund Harrold's account of the consecration I have already quoted. His diary, published by

the late Mr. Harland, embraces a period of some two years—
from the opening of the church, in 1712, to the death of the
queen in 1714. This was a time of comparative quiet. Mr.
Byrom's allusions are limited to the year that followed the disaffection of 1715. This also was a season of apparent stillness.
It will be rather by way of showing the social relations of the
rector with the Collegiate Church, which were invariably friendly,
than to draw political deductions, that we shall quote so freely
from both. Each of these diarists gives us a good idea of
the social life and surroundings of the town at the period of
which he writes. Two men so utterly unlike in thought,
character, and position could not have been found. This is
all the better for our purpose.

Harrold, writing in 1712, says :—

"October 19th: I went both ends to church—heard the little
Nantwich man, and Mr. Ainscough.

"1713, February 14th: Heard Mr. Copley on Watchfulness,
and third sermon on Sobriety. 16th : Fell on drinking all day.
17th : Drank at several places—the 'Goose,' 'Horse and
Dog.' 18th : I was ill in forenoon, but got to church and
heard Dr. Bolton on my Saviour's temptation.

"May 3rd : I heard three sermons, two at Old Church, one
at New (St. Ann's) ; 1st by Dr. Bolton, another by Bishop
Blackley, another by Dr. Band (Bann).

"May 13th : Yesterday was buried Dr. Yarborough, at the
New Church ; Dr. Band (Bann) preached his funeral sermon.
He's the first that ever was buried there.* (This is confirmed
by the register at the Cathedral. I cannot find his grave ;

---

* One of the earliest burials in St. Ann's was that of John Best. His
epitaph runs thus :—"John, son of Luke Best, of Manchester, limner, buried
November ye 7th, 1718." Originally the "enlumineur" was employed in
decorating the title pages of books. The term, in this sense, is now all but
obsolete. In the trades procession at York, in 1415, the "Escriveners" and
"Lumners" marched together. "Nicholas Cotes, lummer," is set down

probably it lies under the pavement outside the present rails, where many memorial tablets still lie beneath the flag-stones.)*

"June 15th: Stayed at home forenoon. Heard Bishop of Man (Sodor and Man) in St. Ann's, afternoon, on 'Peace of Conscience.'

"August 1st: I'm in a miserable condition. (The 'askings' had been put up for his third marriage!) 2nd: I fled to St. Ann's. In forenoon I heard Dr. Leaster there.

"August 16th: Dr. Ainscough told me plain he would not marry me, because I was a madman in drink; that the woman ran her ruin in marrying me. By God's help I will observe these rules:—1, Not to drink any strong drink in the morning; 2, Not above a pint at a sitting of business; 3, As little as possible in public-houses; 4, Keep home with the greatest diligence. Heard Dr. Band (Bann) at St. Ann's, two sermons, one on the 'Sacrament,' the other on 'Sincerity of Intentions.'

"August 19th: Saw Ann—was with her five hours. We concluded to be married in the morning.

"August 20th: But its mist (missed); the reason was she could not get time to-day.

"September 6th: Heard Dr. Seddon at St. Ann's. 20th: Went to St. Ann's; heard Dr. Leaster on 'the Creation of Man.'

"October 23rd: Bless God I've not spent 1d. in ale-house this nine days. 31st: Finished this month well, being sober, constant in duties, public and private, studious and contented.

in the "Corpus Christi Guild," York, a little later on. (Surtees Society.) In "Cocke Lorelles' Bote" mention is made of

" Parchemente makers, skynners, and plowers,
  Barberes, boke-bynders, and lyminers."

The frontispieces of many old books will show how oft the services of the "limner" was resorted to. The monks were great limners, as our missals prove.

* The fourth burial was that of Dr. Banne, the rector's father. "1713—14. January 7. Nathaniel Banne, Dr., at St. Ann's."

"1714, August 3rd : Heard this day of Queen Anne's death ; there's great sorrow for her.

"August 6th : News of King George's proclamation at London, on 1st instant, they say here to-day. Heard King George prayed for at St. Ann's Church this day. O God send us peace.

"August 20th : Drunk King George's health ; and there was bonfires and ringing for his safe arrival in England the 18th instant, at Greenwich, about six at night. (Two days seems to have been the average time for London news to get into the houses of Manchester people).

"September 19–20 : Finished the coronation of King George with lying near two hours in dungeon by Files, constable of Salford ; ill-hurt of face, lost handkerchief, and, indeed, deserve all for being drunk—it shall be last time ever.

"September 21st : As I now think, I'll leave off drink.

"September 22nd : Writ 'Thoughts on Imprisonment.' "

This, I think, will do as a specimen of Edmund Harrold's character, and as a memorial of St. Ann's. He was buried at the old church, on the north side, June 4th, 1721. So early as 1705, I find that as a "perruquier" he had a house in Market-street Lane.

Dr. Byrom, as an old friend, was a frequent attendant at the new church under Mr. Bann's ministry. His chief allusions to the new church embrace the years 1722-1733. It is in these years his diary and letters dwell more particularly on his home life and surroundings. "October 7, 1722. Sunday. New church. Mr. Bann preached ; text, 'Thou shalt not kill.' Afternoon, old church. Mr. Cattell preached ; text, 'Love is the fulfilling of the law.' " This harmonious relation of subjects suggests the thought that Mr. Bann and Mr. Cattell preached in concert. They were great friends ; and the latter being chaplain at the Collegiate Church, probably undertook a share of the daily services at St. Ann's. Then follows a curious

D

statement: " Walked after sermon by the river side by Strangeways with Mr. Leycester and Dr. Mainwaring." They would
pass through the turnstile at Hunt's Bank, and follow the pathway by the stream. How strangely it reads. A ramble by the
Irwell from Hunt's Bank! the fields on either side, thoughtful
converse with two sober-minded divines, one on either side the
author of "Christians Awake." Perchance they shook their heads
as they saw some follower of the gentle craft surreptitiously whip-
ping the stream on the sacred day, somewhere opposite the
present Assize Court! The question now is, not whether the
fish could live in such a polluted stream, but whether the angler
could attempt that same walk and survive the effluvia. It is
an established fact, I believe, that a man not long ago died
from swallowing about a pint of the Irwell, after falling in acci-
dentally. " October 14 (1722). Mr. Sidebotham, of Middleton,*
preached at new church, both fore and after noon." The
worthy doctor seems to have made a constant practice of attending morning prayers on Wednesday. "Wednesday, May
10, 1724. Went to the new church." " Wednesday, Twelfth
Day, 1725. Went to the new church in the morning with
Beppy, and sat in Lady Bland's seat." Dr. Byrom always strove
to preserve his friendship with the foundress. It was not merely
that she was too important a personage to quarrel with ; he met
at Hulme Hall with men and women who, in spite of their opposite political tendencies, were ready enough to acknowledge
his superior mind and to appreciate his conversational gifts.
That he and Lady Bland were friends is undeniable. Almost
immediately he adds : "January 12, 1725. Lady Bland sent
to invite me to the dancing to-night. I walked to Hulme in
the evening, where I found them dancing. We came home
between 12 and 1 in Lady Bland's coach and father Byrom's
chariot, which sister Ann had ordered." These were good
hours for a fashionable ball. "Wednesday, January 20. To-

* Samuel Sidebotham, rector of Middleton from 1714 till 1752.

night Mr. Band (Bann), Samuel and Joseph Clowes, and I, were at Mr. Falconer's, the apothecary's, to supper. We talked about the antiquities of Manchester." "September 5 (1725). Went to the new church with Phœbe. Mr. Cattell preached on 'Peace be with you.'" "1726, January 5, Wednesday. Went to the King's Arms, and passed the night. Vernon, Clowes, Hassel, Mildmay, Sanderson, and I talked about metaphysics, the devil, Balaam's ass, Samson's foxes, and such like matters." Rather hard upon the ass and the foxes!

"1728, August 25, Sunday : Streynsham Master came to Bull's Head as we were going to the new church. Streynsham went to Lyme at night, and I was at Mr. Banne's* with Dr. Malyn, and Mr. Knight." Two years later he is still on good terms, socially, with the Hulme Hall family, but Lady Bland was now old, and alone, and would be glad to see him, I doubt not. On this occasion, however, they met at the Mosley's, of Ancoats. "Nov. 8, 1730 : At Ancoats last night, with Mr. Booth, Lady Bland, Jenny, and Mrs. Lunt. I came home with them in the coach after nine o'clock, and went then to Mr. Lees,† where were Mr. Cranage and Wilson, from

* Mr. Byrom spells the rector's name in four different ways, viz., Band, Ban, Bann, and Banne.

† John Lees, who lived by the conduit in the Market Place. He was the first recorded churchwarden of St. Ann's. He seems to have been a fussy, domineering man, and did not get on very well with his rector, as the following letter will show :—

"Manchester, January 21, 1723-4.

"My Lord,—I suppose that your Lordship hath or will receive from the Churchwardens of ye New Church (St. Anne's,) an account of ye difference betwixt us as to ye disposal of ye offertory-money. That your Lordship might be fully informed, I thought it my duty to acquaint your L'dship with ye case, which is as follows : For several years last past, out of the offertory money, which hath not been counted (as I think it ought to have been), I commonly have taken 3, 4, or 5 shillings to give poor people. The remainder the Churchwardens take. But lately, they thinking that I take too much, or perhaps that I should not take any, on last Sunday,

London." "1733, June 13, Sunday : J. Brooke preached at new church to-day, morning and evening. I was at the old church, morning ; new, afternoon. I have learned how to abound (probably there was a collection). Spoke to Lady Bland."

The next entry carries us back to the celebrated institution of coffee-houses, and throws our mind upon Addison and Steele, the Spectator and the Rambler. Manchester was but a reflection of London. "Sunday : Going to new church in the afternoon, the bell had not begun to ring, so I stepped into St. Ann's coffee-house." St. Ann's had evidently added to

Mr. Lees, ye only Churchwarden then present, w^d not allow me to take any. We counted all ye money, which was about thirty seven shillings, and disposed of none of it. This collection, I believe, was not so great as usual, because ye number of communicants was not so great as at other times. Now, since we disagree, your L^{d}ship is to determine in what method ye offertory money is to be disposed of. People have been very much dissatisfy'd as to what the Churchwardens have had, so that ye collections have not been so great as otherwise they w^d have been. The bottom of all our differences and uneasiness is this. The church is brought into debt by very unnecessary painting about three years agoe : towards ye discharge of which, the Churchwardens, would have ye offertory money apply'd, which I take to be very wrong, as well as ye buying, therewith, some time agoe, by Mr. Lees, without consent of his Brother Church-warden, or mine, a dozen of Common prayer-books for ye use of ye congregation, which cost above four pounds. Mr. Shrigley lately mentioned to me another expedient towards getting ye church out of debt, viz : a Commission from your L^{d}ship, to apply part of ye incomes of ye Rector and Curate to that purpose, which though I suppose impracticable, yet shew'd his good will to us. I am afraid matters will never be easy, and as they should be, among us, till one thing be altered, which I care not to mention without leave, lest I sh^d be thought to pretend to direct your Lordship. I am sorry and ashamed, that I am forced to give your L^{d}ship this trouble for which I humbly ask your L^{d}ship's pardon, I am, my Lord,

Yr L^{d}ship's most dutiful &
most humble servant,
NATH$^{L.}$ BANNE."

The remedy hinted at is evidently the removal of Mr. Lees from the wardenship.

the local nomenclature. There was the "New Church Inn," in Fennell-street, and St. Ann's coffee-house in the Square. *

Nothing can be clearer from these extracts than that the amenities of social life were not allowed to be lost because of political differences. Here I think Dr. Halley has unintentionally fallen into exaggeration. He has ascribed to a period of forty years a state of hostility which was only felt intermittently. There is ever a tendency, in looking back upon our national quarrels, to separate too distinctly their conflictive elements. What is true of a month or year we are apt to make true of an epoch. In such cases as the Sacheverel riots, or the troubles of '15 and '45, this feud was sufficiently fierce to make the several factions stand out most clearly. But when the crisis was over everybody began to settle down into at least an appearance of complaisant good humour. It is so with elections at the present day. For a week there are two hostile camps, and no compromise. Each householder suspects his neighbour across the street of a deliberate attempt to undermine the constitution. But let the poll be declared, and we all gladly subside into a calm again. We shake hands with men we looked daggers at yesterday. Election or no election there must be social intercourse, the conduct of business, and the amenities of life. I am speaking, of course, rather of *party feeling* than party principles. The former is often an institution rather than a sentiment, and like the institution of servants, it must have its occasional day out. One thing is very certain: Manchester, in reality a hot-bed of contending factions, could get on very very comfortably during such times as political or religious excitement was not at fever heat. Awaiting the next *crisis*, Dr. Byrom and Lady Bland, Mr. Bann and Mr. Cattell, Mr. Joseph Clowes and Mr. Marriott—a tremendous king *de facto* man—could meet together and pass an evening pleasantly

* The only trace of this spirit in the present day is found in the "St. Ann's Cigar Company," in the King-street Arcade.

without irritation or distraction of mind. They could discourse upon metaphysics, the devil, Balaam's ass, Samson's foxes, and "such like matters," without the shadow of the Pretender intruding itself to disturb this harmonious sequence of ideas.

Nevertheless, Mr. Bann's position was not an easy one. While Sir William Dawes was his diocesan, he had to deal with a man of like temperament with himself. In 1714 Sir William was made Archbishop of York, and the see of Chester was filled by Dr. Gastrell,* one of the best administrators that diocese has ever seen. Distant as was Manchester from his palace, he took a deep interest in its welfare, and was well acquainted with its political differences. Personally, he was a High Churchman, and a Tory. There is no doubt that he had it in his mind to win over the rector, if not the congregation, to his own views in respect of the Church and the State. One of his earliest acts was to appoint two churchwardens and ten commissioners, to superintend the removal of several abuses which had crept into the church of St. Ann's. By the terms of consecration the choice of wardens and commissioners lay with him. These wardens and commissioners were, with one exception, High Churchmen, most of them habitual attendants at the Collegiate Church. This was sufficient to make Mr. Bann's position a delicate one.

A second act of the Bishop was still more trying, though it came in the form of an honour to the rector. He was appointed one of the Bishop's chaplains. The recent sedition in 1715 had fully shown to his lordship the exact state of parties in the town. He knew that the Collegiate Church was all but wholly with him. It was as equally manifest that St. Ann's was not. The patroness of Low Church views was its

* Bishop Gastrell was one of the earliest supporters of the Christian Knowledge Society. His short work on the Catechism is amongst the first in its catalogue, and is still used.

foundress, and still lived. The chief contributors were the same, and held their pews there. The leading constitutionalists of the town habitually worshipped there. It was, in fact, the acknowledged rendezvous of the Low Church as distinct from the Presbyterian faction. His hope lay in the rector. Nathaniel Bann had been preferred to St. Ann's from the ranks of the Collegiate clergy. He was naturally of a quiet and undemonstrative turn, possibly therefore pliable, or to put it more courteously, open to conviction. He was, and had been for long, the friend of Clayton, Cattell, and Byrom. Might not a chaplaincy make him still more open to conviction? I think that the hope of attaching Mr. Banne to the side of the High Churchmen explains this piece of preferment. The Bishop could meet with his chaplain in the discharge of his new duties, and gain opportunities of attempting his conversion.

Whether it be true or false that these acts of the Bishop had a deeper significance than might appear on the surface, one thing is clear, the congregation resented the character of the commission, and became but more constitutional. The abuses which the commission were to investigate were real. Among the family archives of the late Miss Atherton was found a printed sheet. The paper is yellow with age, but otherwise perfect. It was kindly sent to the present rector by the executors, and now hangs framed in the vestry of St. Ann's. It may be deemed interesting enough to quote entire. A value attaches to it, inasmuch as it once was in the possession of John Byrom.

" At a meeting by the Rector of St. Ann's Church and the Commissioners this Day, held for regulating the Letting of the Seats in the said church, 'tis agreed—

February 2nd, 1718-9.

That no Person whatsoever, on any Pretence, shall alienate his or her seat, altho' a Contributor.

That whatever sittings are Lett in any seat over and above

what is requisite for the Family of the Possessor, shall
be lett by the Rector and Commissioners for the Benefit of the Rector.

That every Person recommended by a Contributor to the
Building of the said Church shall have preference to
all other persons.

That if any Contributor or his Family shall hereafter come
as a hearer, he or she shall enter into and be Tenant
to his or her seat at the First Rent.

That this shall be a standing Rule, and be observed as such
in the Disposal of the seats for the Future.

Signed by

NATHANIEL BANNE, Rector.

WILLIAM SHRIGLEY,* ⎫ Churchwardens and
JOHN LEES,   ⎬ Commissioners.

JOHN LIGHTBOUNE.   JOHN LEECH.
JOHN GREAVES.†   WILLIAM HUNTER. §
JAMES BECK.   DANIEL WOOLMER.
MATTHEW GREAVES.†   SAMUEL BROOKES.
MILES NIELD.‡   JEREMIAH BOWER."‖

* Mr. Shrigley and Mr. Lees are the two first recorded churchwardens.
William Shrigley was an attorney of considerable position in Manchester.
His son, the Rev. William Shrigley, was chaplain of the Collegiate Church,
and died in 1756 at the age of 62. His name is occasionally found in St. Ann's
register about the year 1740, when he seems to have undertaken the daily
services. The father, grandfather, and great grandfather of the churchwarden
were all "William Shrigley," and lived at Ardwick. The father of the chaplain
obtained high eminence in his profession, and was highly respected by the
whole community for his urbanity. All five Williams were buried, I believe, at the Collegiate Church.

† John Greaves and Matthew Greaves were brothers, the sons of
Edward Greaves, an apothecary in the town. In the "Pole Booke,"
1690, his name duly occurs, "Mr. Edward Greaves, Gent., for £200,
wife and five children, Ould Mealegate." From John descended the
Greaves of Culcheth. Matthew, of Manchester, linen draper, was buried
at the Collegiate Church, May 11, 1747, aged 70 years. He was churchwarden at the Collegiate Church in 1713-1714.

No one can doubt that this was a step in the right direction. It nipped a great and growing abuse in the bud so far as St. Ann's was concerned. Nevertheless, being the act of ten commissioners and two churchwardens, all of whom had been set over the heads of the congregation by a Bishop who had little or no sympathy with the latter's views, the whole transaction, no doubt, would be looked upon as a gross piece of tyranny. The crowning wrong was that all these men, save

‡ In the plan of Manchester, dedicated to Lady Bland, and drawn between 1712-1734, Miles Nield's house in Hunt's Bank may be seen. This tallies with Byrom's diary, Manchester, 1738. "Last night died old Mrs. Nield, at the Hunt's Bank." "Sarah, widow of Miles Nield, of Manchester, chapman, buried in the choir, March 14, 1738." (Collegiate Church Register.) Miles Nield was son of Roger Nield, of Manchester (lived 1648-1696). He was born in 1670, and died just before his wife, in 1738. His daughter Elizabeth (1701-1776) married William Clowes, also of Hunt's Bank. The Victoria Station, abutting on the river Irk, occupies the site of both houses. Miles Nield was cousin by marriage to John Byrom. He was churchwarden at the Collegiate Church in 1715 and 1728.

§ William Hunter was co-executor with John Diggles under the will of George Grimshaw, who in 1717 left £1,000, the interest of which was to go to the rector of St. Ann's. James Beck, John Lightbowne, and Daniel Woolmer, all belonged to well-known local families. The Lightbownes lived at Lightbowne Hall, Moston.

‖ Jeremiah Bower was a wealthy hatter, churchwarden of Collegiate Church in 1724, senior constable in 1734, and boroughreeve in 1743. He built a large house in High-street, which had recently come into existence. Here he lived before it was converted into the "Old Bridgewater Hotel," long a celebrated posting-house. (Vide vol. ii. 401, Byrom's Remains.) He died in 1755, and was buried at the old church. On a brass candelabrum in the choir is this inscription, "The gift of Jeremiah Bower, Manchester, haberdasher of hats, September 29, 1745." This was a few days before the Pretender entered the town. Benjamin Bower, his son, born 1731, was senior constable in 1772, churchwarden in 1773, and boroughreeve 1775.

James Beck, were attendants at the Collegiate Church.*
When it is added that the two churches were even now at
discord, the result of the Sacheverel disturbances, we can conceive that this episcopal interference would not be relished by
the seatholders of St. Ann's.   The Sacheverel riot was not yet
more than two years old, and the Whigs and Presbyterians
had not forgotten it.   That riot is but a proof how strong was
the High Church feeling in Manchester.   In no part of the
kingdom had the preacher more determined friends than there.
High Church clergy, Jacobite gentry, Nonjurist tradesmen,
all joined in the cry, and nowhere was it more loudly
raised : " Down with the Whigs, and Sacheverel for ever."
They were helped by the " residuum "—which existed then
as now—for the rabble dearly loves mischief.   The man was
unworthy, but of course that did not matter to the residuum.
As for the higher classes, he was a peg to hang a grievance on,
and it was all the same whether the peg was of gold or brass.
That there was much of the last in Sacheverel's composition
the most bigoted partisan must have been constrained to admit.
The cause of Sacheverel was fanned into a flame.   The
preacher of seditious discourses became the idol of the hour.
His sermons might be burnt, but they were circulated every-
where.   The Tories triumphed, and it was only the queen's
death that prevented the Schism Act from coming into force.
When it was discovered that King George would adhere to the
Toleration Act, the anger of the High Church faction in Manchester knew no bounds.   The fellows and chaplains, and,
doubtless, the " singing men " and " singing boys," were all
of the Pretender's party.   In 1715, on the 10th of June, the
birthday of " James the Third," an active mob paraded the

* Three at least of these commissioners sided with the Tories in their
successful opposition to the workhouse scheme of 1731.   As this was
notoriously a trial of party strength, their action must have made the
Whigs of St. Ann's very sore.—Vide Byrom's Remains, vol. i., p. 440.

streets. Backed by the Jacobites, they proceeded to the chapel in Cross-street, then Pool Fold, smashed its doors and windows, overturned its pews and pulpit, and left the whole place a wreck.* There can be little doubt that had they dared they would gladly have completed their self-imposed task by demolishing the Corinthian fabric, only four years old, that faced the Close. As Dr. Halley says, with but a grain of exaggeration, " the Low Churchmen of St. Ann's had much less of friendly feeling with the High Churchmen of the Collegiate Church, notwithstanding their uniformity of worship, than they had with their neighbours, the Nonconformists of Cross-street." St. Ann's had become familiarised already as the religious rendezvous of the Whigs. Lady Bland was its staunch patroness. The Marriotts and Allens worshipped there. On the 6th August, 1714, George was at once prayed for, as Harrold informs us, as King of England, the day upon which the news of his proclamation arrived. Evidently, Mr. Bann accepted the king *de facto*, whatever views he might have of the king *de jure*. This riot was headed by Thomas Syddall, a peruke maker. He, with several others, was committed to Lancaster for the outrage, and, as everybody knows, was afterwards, through joining the rebels at Preston, again imprisoned, only to come forth to execution in February, 1716.

As years passed on, the High Church party became still more disaffected in the town. The Collegiate Church was practically in their hands. Mr. Byrom lent them his potent influence, though not so openly as many others. It was now his epigrammatic powers shone out—powers that have made him outlive his own, if not all time. He, and Clayton with him, asserted the people's rights to resist an unlawfully established authority. Samuel Peploe, who, by his bold conduct at Preston, had been appointed head of the Collegiate Church, was no match for the poet nor the under clergy; and as he had

---

* The chapel was rebuilt at the cost of the town.

no right to occupy the pulpit, saving on the greater festivals, the fellows and chaplains had it all their own way. Speaking of this period, Dr. Halley says, " Constitutional liberty would have fared ill in Manchester had it not been for the Whig rector and curate* of St. Ann's, and the minister of the Presbyterian meeting-house in Acres Field (Pool Fold). The people were as zealous for their respective parties as were their teachers. Ladies in plaid petticoats, and gentlemen in plaid waistcoats, representing Stuart preferences, frequented the Collegiate Church, except when the warden preached ; while other ladies with orange ribands, and other gentlemen with orange handkerchiefs, worshipped in St. Ann's, or in the Cross-street meeting-house. In the Collegiate Church, when the prayer for King George was mumbled over, the people rose from their knees. In St. Ann's that prayer was repeated with especial emphasis and favour. Such was the religious life of Manchester in the early part of the last century."

The reader will have noticed that I have spoken restrainedly of Mr. Bann's proclivities. To describe him as a public expounder of Whiggism and Low Churchmanship would be a mistake. We should be falling into the error of judging the man by his church, his patroness, and congregation. He had lived too many years in the seclusion of the library to be much of a public partisan. I should judge that the flock at St. Ann's rather led the shepherd than the shepherd

---

* The curate at this time was Mr. Felton. We know him only by his epitaph, for he lies close beside his rector. "Gregory Felton, obiit Nov. 27, anno salutis mdcclxi, ætatis xl. Also Elizabeth, wife of the late Nathaniel Chadwick, of Bolton, and granddaughter of the Rev. Gregory Felton, late minister of this church, who departed this life July 4, 1826, aged 77 years." One single fact is gleaned from the Byrom papers. He married Anne, daughter of the Rev. Egerton Leigh, archdeacon of Salop, who had a house in King-street, one of the first built there. The Leighs, of King-street, were constant attendants at St. Ann's. Several of the family lie buried in the churchyard.

the flock. He was that much maligned individual, a moderate man—one who would sacrifice much for peace. I doubt whether he was a very popular man, either at the new church or the old. In fact, he stood betwixt two fires, and got slightly roasted by both. Lady Bland made him rector of St. Ann's, and so identified him with the Low Church faction. Bishop Gastrell, a rigid and bigoted Tory, appointed him his chaplain, and thus connected him with the High Church phalanx. The Collegiate Church pulled him towards Scotland, Hulme Hall towards Hanover. His friends at the Hospital wore tartan, his associates at St. Ann's were clad in orange. Early associations bound him to Christ Church, still earlier memories clustered round the Presbyterians and Pool Fold. He was in a strait betwixt two. But his Protestantism brought him out unscathed. No one can read his unpublished annotations on the Book of Revelation* without seeing the impossibility of his being otherwise than a Constitutionalist. There he was with his congregation. He was not a demonstrative Whig. He was far too much in love with his books and his meditations to be an active partisan.

That he laboured hard for peace is unquestionable. A man who deliberately sought the services of such men as Mr. Cattell and Mr. Aynscough for his pulpit, both attached to the Collegiate body—a man who at such a time preserved unbroken his friendship with Dr. Byrom and Mr. Clayton, must have longed for peace.

We can understand Mr. Bann's relief when for a time the rage of conflicting parties ebbed. Ere the tide turned he was dead ; human passion could affect him no more. The long reign of peace had, for him, set in. His sermons, we suspect, were somewhat dry—less dry, however, than the age warranted them to be. Probably he was more erudite than edifying ; but even there he was better than his cotemporaries. Had he allowed his

---

* They may be seen in the Chetham's Library.

own mind free play, had he been less in bondage to the school authors, he had doubtless been more popular in the pulpit. But his English was simple, and by speaking strictly in the "vulgar tongue" he was at least understood. He invited John Wesley to occupy his pulpit in 1733—no doubt at Lady Bland's request; she did not die until twelve months after this—and the heart-stirring address of that genuine master of popular appeal reminded him, we can well imagine, of that other preacher whose sweet voice had touched his heart in his childhood, and who, like the founder of the Wesleyan body, ought never to have been allowed to quit the pastures of the English Church.

Nathaniel Bann's distinctive trait was humility, without which no man can preach a true gospel. His guilelessness of purpose, his meekness of manner, were marked. His name had foreshadowed it ; his life had demonstrated it. "Nathanael, verè Israelita," says his epitaph ; but we have something better than epitaphs to fall back upon. Too often the churchyard tablet declares what a man ought to have been rather than what he was ; for the bright torch of charity gleams nowhere brighter than in the chamber of the tomb, and by that light alone is the dead illumined. In the Chetham's Library lies a dusty volume of MSS. of his, styled, "An Answer to Hicke's Constitution of the Catholic Church." This was written in the last year of his life. It is put in the form of a letter. He begins as follows :— "Sir,—I have read, and considered the book you gave me, not without inclination favourable enough to the Party which it defendeth, especially being sufferers. And if the reasons of their conduct were near so plain to me, as by your assurance of their way of writing, I conclude they appear to them, I sh⁴ not by the help of God be backward to stand by ye truth at my utmost peril. But in good earnest the more I read, the less I am satisfy'd, and the reasons of my being so I come now to tell you." He sums up as follows :—"To conclude, why

declarations, signs, actions, gestures, sh^d be necessary to testify
our dissent from offensive prayers, since St. Paul required none
from the sacrificed meats, but only abstaining from it, as I cannot give a good reason myself, so, old as I am, I am willing to
learn and be thankful to my instructor. And if I be in the
wrong about these matters (as I very well may), I beseech God
I may live to see and acknowledge it. May God direct us
into His saving Truth, and guide our feet into the way of
Peace. Amen." We can believe anything good of the man
who wrote these words. They breathe the spirit of "Nathanael
verè Israelita." * In him there could be no guile. No wonder
when he died in 1736, and was laid to rest in front of the vestry
door, there should have been on the slab that covered him
some allusion to his prototype.

" Exuvias hic deposuit Nathanael Banne hujusce ecclesiæ
primus Rector,
literis reconditis apprime eruditus, virtutibus Christianis
mirè ornatus :
amantissimus conjux, pater indulgens, verus-que amicus,
presbyter fidelis,
fide orthodoxus, praxi illustris verus demum Nathanael,
verè Israelita
obiit 9 Septembris, anno salutis 1736, ætatis 65.''

I strongly suspect his life-long friend Mr. Clayton, Fellow of
the Collegiate Church, and for a time rector of Salford, was his
executor. At any rate, it appears to have been through his agency
that Mr. Bann's papers were deposited in the Chetham Library.
The first volume of his everyday book is thus prefaced: " A
very careful abridgement of the very pious and learned perpetual commentary of the Rev. Charles Daubuz, M.A., upon

* Mr. Bann evidently wrote with the intention of publishing his works.
His modesty, however, seems to have stood in the way.

St. John's Revelation.   This epitome was compiled by the
rev. and learned Nathaniel Banne, M.A., rector of St. Ann's
Church, in Manchester, and formerly keeper of Chetham's
Library; and is here deposited as a monument of the learning
and industry of the author, and a testimony of the great regard
he had for the very important work upon which he employed
so much time and pains: not to satisfy the curiosity of idle and
desultory readers, but to incite them to the same diligence in
studying the great work, of which the compiler hath given so
eminent an example: By an intimate friend of Mr. Banne's, as
well as a great admirer of the excellent Mr. Daubuz, *J.
Clayton.*"

That Mr. Bann was married we know, for a daughter,
Catherine, was christened at the Collegiate Church in January,
1722 ; but of his wife and family no trace, to my knowledge,
remains.   Strangely enough, too, there is no epitaph of his
father, the physician, although, as we have already stated, he
was buried in his son's churchyard.   The rector did not long
survive his patroness,* and, with her death and his, the

* A tablet to Lady Bland's memory in Didsbury Church has this inscription :—

    Here lyes ye Body of Ann, Lady Dowager BLAND,
    Sole Daughter and Heiress of Sir EDWARD MOSLEY,
    Of Hulme, Knt. She married Sir John Bland,
    Of Kippax Park in ye County of York, Bart.,
    To whom She brought a plentifull estate
    In this Neighbourhood, and by Whom She had
    A numerous issue, though None of Them surviv'd Her,
    Except a Daughter, MERIELL, married to
    HILDEBRAND IACOB, Esq.,
    And Sir IOHN BLAND, of Kippax Park and Hulme, Bart.,
    Who erected This Monument in Memory of
    One of the best of Women, Anno 1736.

"1734, August 3. Buried D. A. B., *alias* The Honourable Lady Bland,
relict of Sir John Bland, Baronett : died July 26."—Didsbury Chapel, p. 77.

connection of the Bland family with, and their influences upon the church terminate. *

* 1723, August 8. Mr. Adam Bland, at St. Ann's. (Extract from Burials of Collegiate Church.) This Mr. Bland was cousin by marriage to Lady Bland, being the son of Adam Bland, uncle of Sir John. He married Miss Chetham, at Chapel-en-le-Frith, February 28, 1714 (vide Register), and a memorial to his father-in-law, Edward Chetham, by Mr. Clowes and Mr. Bland may still be seen in the private chapel of the Chetham family at the Collegiate Church. Adam Bland lies close to the first rector, near the vestry door of St. Ann's. He is the sole member of the Bland family buried there. His daughter Mary was christened at the Collegiate Church, " 1717, December 19, Mary, daughter to Mr. Adam Bland."

E

III.

JOSEPH HOOLE,

1736–1745.

THE second rector of St. Ann's, Joseph Hoole, is first presented to us as the personal friend of Mr. Byrom, the poet, already mentioned several times, he who wrote that epigram, the last couplet of which has been quoted as often as any two lines in Shakspere :

> Strange all this difference should be
> 'Twixt tweedle-dum and tweedle-dee.

That for more than a century these lines should have been attributed to Dean Swift* we can forgive, for this is not the least of the Manchester epigrammist's compliments. John Byrom was born in 1691, and sent to Chester to school, and from thence to Merchant Taylors, in London. From this seminary he went to Trinity College, Cambridge, and there sat scholastically under the great Bentley. Until he came into the Kersal property by the death of his elder brother he taught a system of steno-graphy, which took him constantly to London, although he generally whiled away a few days on the road at his Alma Mater. His letters and diary are now published. There is

---

* "Elegant Extracts," so popular with our youth at the close of the last century, first stereotyped this error.

good reason for believing not only that Joseph Hoole owed his appointment to John Byrom, but that the two were connected by marriage.

The first mention of Mr. Hoole is found in a letter dated March 31, 1733, written by J. Garden, nephew of a celebrated mystic religionist, to the "Rev. Mr. Hoole," from Normanby. In it he says, "I am glad you have found so good conversation as Mr. Byrom's. Few people in England are better acquainted with the gentlemen that are admirers of the mystic divinity than I am. I should be mighty proud of seeing you and Mr. Byrom together, and then we should talk freely on this subject." This note is addressed to the "Rev. Mr. Hoole, at Haxey."*

A few months later we find Mr. Byrom staying with his new friend. He dates a letter to his wife from Haxey, October 19, 1733 ; a letter, by the way, of peculiar quaintness. He describes his journey from Manchester, his drinking of the waters at Buxton, his calling at Chatsworth. Thence he passed on by coach into Lincolnshire, and reaching the rectory at Haxey, writes, "Mr. Hoole sends you his service." A few days later he arrived at Cambridge. Dating a second letter from Trinity College, October 27, he says, "My dear, this is the first opportunity of writing to thee since I writ from Haxey by Mr. Horbury. I stayed there till Monday, and Mr. Hoole would go with me to Lincoln, and next day to Ancaster." A month later he writes, "My service to Mr. Hoole. I am glad he is got well home. I was very happy in his good company. I will write unto him ere long." From this it would appear that Mr. Hoole had written to Manchester on his return to Haxey, probably not knowing Mr. Byrom's address in London. All this proves a close intimacy between the two, before Mr. Hoole came to Manchester as rector of St. Ann's.†

The new rector was probably first introduced to Mr. Byrom,

---

* *Byrom's Remains, I. 519.*   † *Byrom's Remains, I. 530.*

as in the case of so many other friends, through seeking his tuition in the art of shorthand. In November, 1739, proposals were made "to print by subscription a New Method of Shorthand, by John Byrom, M.A., sometime Fellow of Trinity College, Cambridge." Amongst the signatures of gentlemen who recommended the publication are found those of Charles Wesley, Peter Leigh, Esq., Mr. John Lees, and "Rev. Mr. Joseph Hoole, rector of St. Ann's, Manchester." It seems natural to find one of our greatest, if not the greatest, of English hymn writers, the brother of John Wesley, in such close relationship to him who some years after this wrote the most popular if not the most inspired of Christmas anthems, "Christians, awake, salute the happy morn." This hymn is at times clumsy, halts frequently, and in reality is only redeemed by its peculiar quaintness and simplicity. These two latter qualities, however, perfectly harmonise with the season commemorated ; and as the hymn was eminently adapted for midnight minstrels, the "wakes" being perhaps more established in Lancashire than any other county in England, its popularity was immediate and still remains. To begin the Christmas service in our Lancashire churches without Byrom's hymn, to Wainwright's tune, would be to disconnect Christmas from its most sacred memories ; it would cause a small religious riot.

Joseph Hoole, of Sidney Sussex College, Cambridge, where he took his Master's degree "per literas regias," was vicar of Haxey, in Lincolnshire, when first introduced to us as the Manchester poet's acquaintance. He was senior to his friend, and over fifty before he came northwards. While in Haxey he had made himself known in ecclesiastic circles by a work entitled, "An admonition to churchwardens, exciting them to a discharge of their duty, and answering the pretences that are made for the neglect of it.—St. Matt. v. 33, by Joseph Hoole, vicar of Haxey. London, printed for W. and J. Innys, in St. Paul's Churchyard, mdccxxvii." The tone of this book is sufficiently stern and exhortatory, but there can be no doubt such a work was needed, the laxity of the times, and the absence of a sense of responsibility on the part of officials requiring a strong and severe, if not harsh hand to deal with them.

As already intimated, it was owing to John Byrom that Mr. Hoole came to St. Ann's. The new rector was no stranger to the place. His family had originally sprung from the county, and he must have had relatives or friends in Manchester many years before he came to reside there.* A son Richard, aged eight years, lies buried in the same grave with the rector, yet he had died nearly four years before his father received the incumbency. An incident relating to Mr. Hoole's connection with Haxey is found in one of Byrom's letters. Writing April 11, 1737, a few months after the appointment to St. Ann's, he says, "He (Mr. Garden, Hoole's non-juring friend), said that Mr. Hoole had said that my children were the finest, prettiest children he had ever seen. (Mrs. Hoole was not present evidently). I said that Mr. Hoole saw everything in the best light, and was too partial to his friends ; that though I thought well of my children as being my own, yet that there were much finer. He (Mr. Garden) told me that Mr. Hoole's brother having been to the Archbishop of York for the living of Haxey, the Archbishop said that he wondered at his brother's assurance and at his impudence, and, hark ye, Mr. Hoole had laid out £1000 at Haxey, and had built the house there." If true, this was somewhat strong language for an archi-episcopal utterance,

* This is further, almost finally confirmed by the fact that in the subscription volume of Mr. Hoole's sermons, printed after his death, there occurs the name of "Thomas Houghton Hoole, of Wanstead, two sets." The subscription of Mr. Houghton, Baguley, Lancashire, almost immediately follows. Houghton was and is a well-known Lancashire name. In the Houghtons of Baguley we may see further influences brought to bear upon Mr. Hoole's appointment. Probably his mother was a Houghton. In this case Mr. Hoole would be connected by marriage with John Byrom himself, for Miss Byrom speaks of " Uncle Houghton," of Baguley.

but we may discount it to a certain extent by remembering that
Mr. Hoole's brother had gone all the way to York in hopes of
the preferment, and had come away a disappointed man.   As
for the compliment about the children, Mr. Hoole was no worse
nor better a flatterer than men and clergymen have been in
every age. They say the nearest way to an Englishman's heart
is through his stomach ; give him a good dinner.   This I suspect refers to bachelors.   A rival path at least lies through his
children.   The compliment here given was fulsome enough,
but Mr. Byrom evidently stomached it, and when he passed it
on, as he was bound to do, to Mrs. Byrom, no doubt she
stomached it even better than he. We can only trust, though it
matters little by this time, that Mr. Hoole's lavish praises never
reached Mrs. Hoole's ear.   The new rector at this very time
had two young children of his own !

Several changes are to be noted at this time.   Locally Sir
Oswald Mosley had erected an Exchange in 1729, not far from
the site of the present edifice, while in 1735 the south side of
Acres Field began to be built upon, and King-street, so called
from the second George, and Ridgefield too, were beginning to
become substantial realities.   But as they were surrounded
with gardens, the aspect was still rural enough.   With the
appointment of Mr. Hoole, the register of births, deaths, and
marriages was kept at the home church.*   The Collegiate
Church voluntarily forewent its prerogative.   Their own surplice
duty was quite large enough by this time, and had they foreseen
the chaplain's work at the font and communion rails a generation

---

* One of the first entries at the home church runs: " Dorothy Rockaby,
commonly called Nurse Scarborough, was buried September 20, 1743."
It is hard to know which was her real name.   If she was a professional
nurse or midwife, it would be a curious coincidence that " Rockaby" should
be her patronymic, " Rock-a-by baby, on a tree top" being as popular in
the nursery then as now.   Evidently her nickname, whichever it may be,
was connected with the rhyme.

after this, they would have been even more startled.* The first entry at St. Ann's is dated December 11, 1736. The third entry of baptism is that of "Hannah, daughter of Rev. Joseph Hoole, and Sarah, his wife," who was baptised January 6th, 1737. Thus we see that the new shepherd had begun an increase of his flock at an early period of his pastorate.

A week after this we find Mr. Byrom's first reference to Mr. Hoole as rector. January 14, 1737, Thursday : " Came from Kersal, where I went yesterday, having been ill of rheumatism (his elder brother resided at the Cell). Mr. Hoole at the library (Chetham), and none else but Mr. Thyer.† I went with Mr. Hoole in my boots to the new church (the boots refer perhaps to the rheumatism). Mr. Ward read prayers, Mrs. Byrom and Tedy there."

Again, on Thursday, December 22, in the same year, he writes : " Mr. Hoole drank tea with me this afternoon. Mrs.

---

* By this arrangement St. Ann's was finally made independent of the Collegiate Church. There could be no absolute rupture between the two churches so long as this compulsory connection existed. The hostility of both, either to other, was infinitely more serious in 1745 than 1715. It must be attributed in great part to the dissolution of the only tie that bound them together.

† This Mr. Thyer was librarian at the Hospital. He married *Silence* Leigh, widow of John Leigh, Archdeacon Egerton Leigh's brother. Her mother was *Silence* Beswicke, daughter of the rector of Radcliffe. *Defiance* was a feminine baptismal name in Manchester at this same time. Both sprang from a custom then dying out, of styling a child by the name of some abstract quality. *Defiance* reminds us of such Puritan names as *Accepted, Abstinence, Increase, Experience, Thanks, Lamentation, Remembrance,* or *Desire.* I have met with all these forms in old registers. *Accepted* Frewen, son of a Presbyterian minister, died Archbishop of York. He had a brother " *Thankful* Frewen." A curious entry is found in St. Ann's register of baptisms, May 27, 1805. " *River*, son of *River* and Rebecca Jordan." River Jordan, the son, lies buried in Prestwich churchyard. I may add here that the Cathedral registers of 1793 record the marriage of John *Ghost* to Mary *Sexton*.

Byrom went to Strangeways with Mrs. Mainwaring and her sister Ann. I asked Mr. Hoole if he had read Jac. Behmen, and he said it was unintelligible to him as he read, that he had been told he was an enthusiast, and I talked away in my usual old strain : He asked me to read Dr. Waterland upon the VI. of St. John, and I said that I would : He said the doctor understood it to mean something that even heathens could partake of, a general way of saying that except ye partake of the atonement of the Son of God ye cannot be saved, which I approved of so far."

That Mr. Hoole was a great admirer of Dr. Waterland will be seen from the fact that two years later he published a communicant's guide to the Eucharist, embodying in it that learned divine's estimate of the sacrament. There are prayers also appended. Indeed it is one of the first of those books of devotion now so common, intended for use by the communicant during the pauses in the service. It is styled, "A Guide to Communicants ; or, the Common Christian instructed in the Doctrine of the Eucharist. Being an extract out of Dr. Waterland's review of that doctrine. By way of Question and Answer. With Devotions for the use of Communicants. By Joseph Hoole, M.A., rector of St. Ann's, in Manchester. London : printed for W. Innys and R. Manby, at the West End of St. Paul's ; and J. Hodges, at Manchester. MDCCXXXIX."* Mr. Hoole seems to have had some personal acquaintance with Dr. Waterland. He concludes the preface by saying : " I have only further to observe that the great author of the Review was acquainted with my design, had these papers laid before him, approved of them, and was pleased to encourage

* I have only seen one copy of this work. It is preserved in the Chetham Library, although it is not set down in the catalogue. On the fly leaf is written : " This book may be termed a companion to that written by the Rev. John Clayton (Bann's friend), in 1745. The title of his book is : Friendly Advice to the Poor. Printed in Manchester by J. Harrop, 1755. J. S."

the publication." Bishop Van Mildert, writing of Bishop Hoadley's " Plain Account," printed in 1735, says : " Dr. Waterland's ' Review' followed early in 1737 : no long interval of time for so extensive and elaborate performance : a work of established reputation both here and abroad, for which he had been collecting materials during a considerable portion of his life."* The Bishop of Durham is not alone among theologians of the nineteenth century who have expressed their admiration of this work. Mr. Hoole, too, has only pronounced a judgment which modern opinion has confirmed.†

It is high time to speak of the rector's views. He was a moderate High Churchman, more or less a Sacramentarian, and a staunch Protestant. Like his predecessor he took little active interest in the affairs of State. It was not till the exigencies of 1744 and 1745 demanded an explicit and decided action that he pronounced himself distinctly as a Constitutionalist and a Whig. Nevertheless, so early as 1724, while yet at Haxey, and a comparatively young man, he avowed himself by implication to be a warm supporter of the reigning house. Dedicating his first work to the Archbishop of York, himself a Whig, he says, " Books are seldom read with much regard that come from private and unknown writers. But when it is seen in the very

* Review of Dr. Waterland's life and writings. William Van Mildert, 1823—p. 218.

† " The general design is briefly stated in the introduction. It was to guard the doctrine of the Sacrament against a *superstitious* abuse of it, on the one hand, and against *profane neglect* of it on the other. Hooker's observation that the Holy Communion is " instrumentally a cause of the real participation of Christ, and of life in His body and blood," is adopted by our author as comprising the substance of the whole doctrine." (Van Mildert, p. 218. Edit. 1823). Mr. Mark Pattison, in his Essay on the Tendencies of Religious Thought in England, observes that the genuine Anglican in constructing his Catena Patrum closes his list with Waterland, and leaps at once to 1833 and the Tracts for the Times, just as Charles II. dated his reign from his father's death.

entrance that they are published with the countenance of so
great a Judge as your Grace is universally known and allowed
to be; so steady and sincere a friend to the Established Church,
and so diligent and zealous a promoter of loyalty and fidelity to
the present Government—this will guard them from the prejudice of parties and recommend them to that notice and kind
reception which will give them an opportunity of doing that
service which is sincerely intended by the author."   Of course
this is very fulsome, but Joseph Hoole was no better and no
worse than any other writer of his day who looked to *patronage*
to sell his book, before the modern puffing system had been
invented.   Some of the finest literary works of the last century
are prefaced with compliments to the patron thereof, which
would make an angel blush to receive. One wonders the patron
did not grasp the kneeling author by his wig, and bid him
"stand up, for I also am a man." This dedication, however, is
sufficient proof of Hoole's political views.   But he was not a
politician.   He was too seriously in earnest about the spiritual
life of his people, as demonstrable by their attendance upon
moral duties, to give much heed to their political proclivities.
He was a strong believer in the Church of England, her orders
and constitution, as an instrument to raise the masses.   To lay
down the law of Church government, to defend the Church's
doctrine, to rebuke laxity of Church discipline, to make the
sacraments one of the main channels of divine grace ; this was
his daily, nay hourly, thought and purpose.   Thus he gave little
mind to his country's politics, even though those politics were
largely tinged with issues that concerned the well-being of the
external Church.   Throughout his " Address to Parents," at
Haxey, in 1724,* his "Exhortation to Churchwardens," in 1727,

---

* This address is dedicated to Sir William Dawes, Archbishop of York.
This is far the best and most careful of Mr. Hoole's works.   The Archbishop saw the MSS. and himself recommended their publication.   The
necessity of seeing children religiously educated is the subject mainly dwelt
upon.

his "Guide to the Eucharist," in 1739, and even in his "Sermons," published after his death in 1747,* there is traceable one leaven, a yearning to quicken Church life in an age that was only just recovering from a long stagnancy. It was this doubtless that drew him and John Byrom into such close association, and linked them in a friendship that variance on political creeds could in no degree snap asunder. The great epigrammist attended his ministry even more frequently than that of his predecessor. Joseph Hoole was true to the throne, else he could not have counted Mr. Marriott, Mr. Allen, and Mr. Baldwin among his congregation. Mr. Lewthwaite and Mr. Nicholls would not have consented to be his curates. He is never found with the fellows of Christ Church talking mild or serious Jacobitism over private tables. It is not charged against him, as against Assheton, that he would not baptise any child at the font by the name of "George." It is not related of him, as of Clayton, that he openly prayed for Charles Edward in the street, or abetted him, like Shrigley,† in the pulpit. With all this he had no sympathy. A zealous, earnest, God-fearing Churchman, the name at the font was nothing, the rite was everything. To establish the throne of the King of kings in the heart of the people committed to his charge was to him a duty so paramount

---

* Among the subscribers to this work are Mr. Samuel Baldwin, of Manchester, Mrs. Katharine Baldwin, ditto, and the Rev. Mr. Baldwin, of Holland, Lancashire. Mrs. Baldwin was granddaughter of Dr. Lamplugh, who, while Bishop of Exeter, befriended James II. One of the king's latest acts was to make him Archbishop of York. His grandson, the Rev. Thomas Lamplugh, rector of Bolton Percy and canon of York, frequently came to Manchester, as Byrom's letters show. He also subscribed to Mr. Hoole's work. As the worshipper at St. Ann's enters the church from the King-street arcade he will tread over the following defaced epitaph :—
" . . . Mary Lamplugh, daughter of . . . Lamplugh, D.D., and granddaughter of Arch . . . Lamplugh . . . her sister Katharine married to Samuel Baldwyn, d. 1777, aged 82 years."
† William Shrigley, chaplain at the Collegiate Church, was son of William Shrigley, Mr. Bann's churchwarden at St. Ann's.

that the fact that a claimant to an earthly kingdom was setting up a standard in front of the north door of his church had by comparison an infinitesimal interest. That much abused text, " My kingdom is not of this world " had sufficient significance to him to make him centre his thoughts, words and works upon his parish, and nought else. Joseph Hoole was a good man.

Nevertheless, the rector was an Englishman, and parsons are but human. The day came, scarce two months before his death, when he was compelled to lift his voice against rebellion at large, and the disaffection of the town. The cloud that overhung the English horizon began to lower. The tide of local politics began to ruffle. The old spirit of strife was still strong, although sleeping. Thirty years back the town had been stirred to its inmost depths by the advances upon the throne made by the first Pretender. The young Chevalier was now in the field, abetted by France, who, however little she cared for the Stuarts as a family, was not sorry to give England something to occupy her attention with while she followed up her own schemes. Many of the sympathisers of '15 were still alive in Manchester, the Jacobite breath had not left the body ; and if some veterans of disaffection were gone, others had inherited their spirit, and were ready to risk much for the Prince. Everybody is familiar with the story ; there is no Manchester man who does not know something about the history of his town in the eventful '45. The supporters of the second plot were comprised of the old three classes, the leading gentry, the Collegiate clergy (saving Dr. Peploe, the new warden), and the non-jurors, headed by the celebrated Dr. Deacon, whose tomb and strange epitaph may still be seen in the north-east corner of St. Ann's churchyard. This second attempt of the Stuarts was made with far more spirit than the first ; it threw England into a state of agitation, and in Manchester its effect for the moment was very powerful. The Prince advanced from the north in November, 1745, taking Lancaster, Preston, and Wigan in his way.

Here he made a halt ; his affairs did not prosper as he anti-
cipated. It was thought advisable to test the feeling of the
town before he entered. The sergeant, accompanied by a
drummer and a singing girl, reached Manchester on the 28th,
and carried the town with the panic they created rather than the
devotion they inspired. For in good sooth all was disappointment for Charles Edward; the enthusiasm was noisy, but it was
forced. There was a crowd about him, but it was one composed of those who would be on-lookers, rather than participa-
tors ; curious spectators, rather than devoted adherents. Money
was raised, but it was a levy rather than a subscription. The
Townleys, poor " Jemmy Dawson," Syddall the younger, and
parson Coppock, did their best to fan a flame, but there was
little fuel to keep up the fire, and they burnt themselves. The
fact is, Manchester was not the Manchester of '15 ; Manchester
had become a town of commercial note ; its inhabitants were
getting on in the world ; the great majority of its people had
no desire for fighting ; warp and weft don't progress in time of
war ; even the Catholics and non-jurors found a difficulty in
raising their partisans.

Nevertheless great dismay was caused among the Constitutionalists, the Low Church party, and the Presbyterians ; even
the Tories deemed it advisable to keep their families as much
as possible out of the way. Mr. Byrom's eldest daughter writes,
"Thursday, September 26 (two full months before the Prince
reached the town). The gentlemen (the Jacobite gentry) are
gone to subscribe at Preston. News is come that the rebels have
beat Sir John Cope on the 21st." Again she writes, "October 8.
My uncle Houghton's birthday, went to Baguley with cousin
Briercliffe, Mr. Cattell, Mr. Thyer, Mr. Greaves, Mr. Egerton,
my papa and mama ; stayed two nights. Everybody in hiding
for fear of the rebels. Two regiments gone through the town.
Mr. Hoole, Mr. Nicholls, Mr. Lewthwaite, preached against
rebellion (at St. Ann's.) My papa and uncle Houghton wrote

after the last (took down his sermon), and he (Mr. Lewthwaite) left off before he had half done (terrified at possible results if the Prince on his arrival should be informed of it). They came again the Sunday after and wrote, but he had made his sermon again (altered it). The Presbyterians are sending everything that's valuable away, wives, children, and all, for fear of the rebels."

These quotations give us a capital insight into the state of affairs. The clergy of St. Ann's, at least, had no sympathy with the second Pretender. The two curates were strongly opposed to the Prince, though Mr. Nicholls had infinitely more spirit than his brother assistant. His two sermons against the rebellion, one in 1745, the other in the following year, were so acceptable to the Whig party that they were printed and circulated. The rector, too, in spite of his somewhat high proclivities, had raised his voice against these coming troubles. His illness that followed must have been sudden and brief, for within five weeks of Mr. Lewthwaite's second discourse he was dead. While the drummer was beating a tattoo on the 28th he lay in his coffin, and the night Charles Edward slept at Mr. Dickinson's, in Market-street Lane, he lay in far more peaceful slumber in the churchyard of St. Ann's. Mr. Byrom's Jacobitism was under the control of a very cautious possessor. His conduct in 1745 is that of a man who had no desire to get into a scrape by demonstrative action in anyone's behalf, least of all the Pretenders. His political faith was not so ungovernable as not to be subservient to his personal and family interests. His epigram of this date is to a certain extent an embodiment of his real feeling:

> God bless the King! I mean our Faith's Defender,
> God bless—no harm in blessing the Pretender!
> But who Pretender is, and who is King,
> God bless us all, that's quite another thing!

Probably, as with many another man at this time, Mr.

Byrom had been contending for a principle rather than a person, and the more he heard of Charles Edward and the nearer he drew to his neighbourhood, the more inclined he felt to be content with the monarchy as it stood. His daughter, at least, had no scruples in calling the northern army "rebels" while peril was at hand. When the crisis was past, and there was no further fear that any member of the family might be beheaded for treason, she seems to have fallen back again into a sentimental devotion to the Prince's cause.

Mr. Hoole died on the 27th November. He was buried on the morning of the 29th. There can be little doubt that this hurry was caused by the fact that the Pretender was already on his way to the town. A few hours delay and the square would be crowded with a mixed and turbulent multitude. The richer householders had already removed their families into the country. Even furniture had been transplanted to places of more assured safety. If the rector's house lay in King-street, or Ridgefield, or the Square—one of these it must have been—it was quite manifest that amid such a jostling and excited crowd, much distress might be caused to the bereaved mourners; nay, it was quite possible that the conduct of the funeral might become an impossibility. By the advice of the wardens, and other friends, Mrs. Hoole determined to bury her husband in the early morning. She was just in time, and no more. The incident has become historic. Attended by the relatives of the deceased, the wardens, and a few members of the congregation, among whom doubtless would be Mr. Marriott, Mr. Allen, and Mr. Baldwin, the bier was borne out of the north door, and the train slowly wended its way to the east end, where the rector's son Richard already lay. At this precise moment a few of the Pretender's officers in their plaid sashes entered the square. Attracted by the procession they drew near, and either from instinctive reverence for the dead, or with an idea of obtaining the favour of the living, they passed through the open

gate, unbonneted, and joined devoutly in the service. White
cockade and black scarf were at one in the presence of death.
Many a white cockade was laid equally low ere a month was
gone.

The mourners at once separated, but many of the townspeople lurking in the rear of the market place had seen the act.
It helped to fan the momentary enthusiasm, and when the
prince himself entered the town, four hours later in the day,
and took up his quarters in Market-street Lane, he was not
merely proclaimed king, but bonfires were lit, the streets
illuminated, and an additional force of three hundred men
furnished from the ranks of the Nonjurists and Jacobites. Each
was presented with the customary cockade, which cost little,
and the promise of five pounds, which cost less. The prince was
put up at Mr. Dickenson's, from which time the house took the
popular title of "the palace." Local nomenclature still marks
the spot.

Mr. Waller, of Ridgefield, who had a pew at St. Ann's, and
who probably would have been at the funeral but for his
duties as boroughreeve, was forced to act the unwelcome part of
medium between the prince and the townsfolk. Mr. Clayton
more willingly prayed in the streets, and preached in the
church in the Pretender's behalf. Young parson Coppock was
appointed chaplain to the army. Three of Dr. Deacon's sons
were among the officers, and Thomas Syddall, son of the
unfortunate peruke-maker who was executed for his share in the
rebellion of 1715, was made adjutant; and "Jemmy" Dawson
was honoured with a captaincy. We need not say much upon
this matter. Their after doings are part of the country's
history. Some of them were noble spirits, and were quite
willing to forfeit their lives for the prince. This forfeit was
rigorously exacted. The progress of the rebel army was
disastrous and brief. A retrograde movement from Derby
quickly ensued. The new recruits deserted on every side, and

though a fair number followed the Pretender to Culloden, their spirit lagged. Coppock, "Bishop of Carlisle," in gown and cassock, was hanged, drawn, and quartered on the 18th of October. The heads of Thomas Deacon and Syddall were exhibited on the Exchange, reverenced with bared heads by some, hooted at by others.

A curious legend got abroad, owing to the incident we have recorded. A story was bruited that St. Ann's possessed a peal of bells, but in consequence of their having rung in the Pretender, they were condemned to perpetual silence—one only was in future to be used for parochial needs. We need not trouble to refute this fable, but the present rector has often been seriously questioned as to the truth of the story. The bell had been rung indeed on that eventful morn, but it was a knell for the departure of the dead, not a peal for the coming of the living. If any political significance could be attached to such an incident it must have been sadly prophetic of the failures and deaths that were to ensue. Nevertheless many people of an antiquarian turn have been known to climb up into the belfry, to behold with expectant eye these *brazen*-faced recusants of that loyalty of which Manchester is now so justly proud. Disappointment has met each. There is one bell, and *a great quantity of dust*. Rust is the proverbial consequence of disuse, and if this dust represent all that now remains of these tongue-tied wretches, we can only see therein the untimely fate that awaits all traitors,—and may all the Queen's enemies come to the same ignominious end.

It is impossible to say in what circumstances Mr. Hoole left his widow; but the fact that two volumes of his sermons were published by subscription three years after his death seems to argue that she was not over well provided for. It is expressly stated that they were printed "for his widow," and probably they were edited by her brother-in-law. We must frankly own that they are unsatisfactory reading—not that they

F

are unorthodox, far from it—but they are intolerably dull. There is not a sparkle of humour, not a touch of quaintness to redeem them. They are not even edifying, for dull sermons may be that. They are written from first to last at a dead-level of long-drawn verbosity. We do not believe this was Mr. Hoole's fault altogether. That he wrote the sermons there can be no doubt, but that the selection from his MSS. was the worst possible, and intentionally so, we are equally sure. Books published for authors' widows, we need not say, are usually for *her* benefit, not the reader's ; and only a good subscription list printed at the beginning can secure much for her. The editor of these sermons had a difficult task. He had to select a certain number of discourses, say thirty, which should be absolutely colourless. To avoid hurting anybody's feelings they must appeal to nobody's feelings. The list of names prefacing the publication, representing every party, and therefore representing the common sympathy, and nothing more, fully shows that if the subscribers were to be kept in good humour, the sermons must be of a pointless character. Every preacher has plenty of vapid, comma-less, sermons somewhere in his desk. Some of the best preachers in England have preached some of the poorest sermons in England. It was Mr. Hoole's fate, however, that the interests of his widow demanded that his feeblest thoughts, pictured in his weakest moments and penned in his dullest style, should be chosen for the public perusal. Mr. Byrom's copy is remarkably clean, though it is 130 years old. We feel assured he never read more than ten pages of it. It is absolutely painful to compare the Rector's Address to Parents in 1724 with these sermons put forth in 1748. We could quote page after page of the former with an assurance that the reader would read, mark, learn, and inwardly digest them. For our worst enemy we could wish no sterner punishment than a compulsory perusal of any fifty pages throughout the two volumes of the latter. As is the manner of all poor discourses, these are inordinately long. . It requires great ability to preach a short sermon. We have no doubt that in his happier moments Mr. Hoole could think tersely, write pointedly, and speak briefly. Nevertheless, glancing over these discourses, our last thought as somnolence steals upon us, is that our forefathers were a patient and long-suffering race—on Sundays.*

After her husband's death, Mrs. Hoole seems to have gone to London.† Mr. Byrom continued his interest in the widow of his friend. Writing to Mrs. Byrom on one of his journeys, August 3, 1749, he says, " I thank you for Mr. Hoole's buffet ;

* I remember well, when about ten years old, staying with some friends in Derbyshire, and attending a service held in a barn. The nearest church was three miles off. The preacher was a kindly and venerable-looking gentleman, without a vestige of capillary protection. Immediately above his head hung a shallow sconce with a tall candle. He discoursed for fully an hour without let or hindrance. But his punishment came. The barn was full of draughts, the candle "swealed" dreadfully, the sconce filled. With fascinated eye I watched the inevitable catastrophe. Suddenly a little rivulet of molten grease descended with a run upon the smoothest cranium I have ever seen. The acrobatic performance that followed is indelibly fixed on my memory. The preacher, failing to recover himself, could not be expected to recover his discourse, and the sermon collapsed.

† Mrs. Hoole had a son, about twenty-one years old at his father's death. He lived to be Vice-President of Magdelene College, Oxford. His admission into the Manchester Grammar School is dated August 8, 1737, "Joseph, son of Joseph Hoole, of Manchester, clergyman." Mr. Smith says, "He matriculated at Brazenose College, Oxford, 17th March, 1741, aged seventeen ; elected demy of Magdelene College, July 1743 ; took degree of B.A., November 13th, 1744 ; M.A., 20th June, 1747 ; was elected fellow of the college in the same year; and proceeded B.D., May 25th, 1754. He held the following offices at Magdelene College : Junior Dean of Arts, 1754 ; Bursar, 1755, 1765, 1772 ; Vice-President, 1764 ; Dean of Divinity, 1766. He was presented by the college to the rectory of Winterbourne Bassett, Wilts, March 31, 1773 ; and died 4th February, 1783."—For *Maxey* in Mr. Smith's reference to his father, read *Haxey*; an evident mistake of the printer's.

a worse might have served, but as it was his, it is so much the better.   I had a great value for him, and shall be glad to see Mrs. Hoole.   Does she stay here? (London).   Where may one find her?"   A fortnight later he writes, "I called at the Angel in Bishopsgate-street to see Mrs. Hoole on Friday evening, but she was gone out."   Again a week later he says—we might as well write the letter in full.   "August 26, 1749.   My dear, dear love.   I have been all day preparing to go in the coach that came from Manchester, but on calling to-night at the Axe Inn,* I find that some Irish family has hired it to go to Chester.   I had some talk with the honest coachman, and perceive that it was hired before he came hither, as they look'd out for customers beforehand, so that I must look out for some other opportunity.   I went again to enquire for Mrs. Hoole, but she was out of town.   Yesterday morning she called at Abington's with Miss and her niece, and I went with her to show her the way from my lodgings to Gloucester-street, and then went to enquire about other matters.   I met her this evening in Gray's Inn as I was going to the Axe (Inn) after a visit, and took my leave, making no doubt but that I should go down on Monday, but it happened otherwise.   I must take the next opportunity of which I shall advertize thee, and am in the meantime Thine, thine, thine, etc., etc.   To Mrs. Eliz. Byrom, near the Old Ch., in Manchester, Lancashire."†   This is a fair specimen of the old-fashioned gallantry of husbands to their wives not much more than a century ago.

* Probably the old Axe Inn mentioned a century earlier (1634) by Drunken Barnaby:

> Country left I in a fury,
> To the Axe in Aldermanbury
> First arrived, that place slighted,
> I at the Rose in Holborn 'lighted.

† *Byrom's Remains, II. 504.*

Mr. Hoole's epitaph runs as follows :—" Hic jacet spe carnis resurrectionis, die supremo Josephus Hoole, A.M. Hujusce ecclesiæ Rector. Qualis erat dies iste indicabit, Obiit 27 Novembris Anno Salutis 1745, ætatis 63." He is buried close beside his predecessor, Nathaniel Bann.

IV.

ABEL WARD,

1745-1785.

HE history of the first two rectors of St. Ann's is a curious record. The least observant of readers must have detected the influence of the Jacobite poet upon the Hanoverian clergy. John Byrom was a man of enchantments. Lady Bland had built St. Ann's expressly to rid herself of such as he, yet he comes to the church, worships, and goes back to tea with her in her own coach. Nathaniel Bann is the son of Henry Newcombe's warmest friend, is to the dowager a kind of foster child, yet his most pleasant hours are wiled away in the company of the epigrammatist. The election of his successor is practically controlled by the influence of the same individual. Both men, to an appreciable extent, were as clay in his hands. Without moulding them to his principles, he biassed their practice. He could not turn them into Jacobites, but he took the sting out of their Whiggism. He patronised both, and both were unconsciously proud of it. Only when the political storm actually burst upon their heads did they recognise their peril, and attempt to shake off this pleasant tyranny. I do not think that this power of John Byrom has been fully represented. He must have been terribly fascinating.

But there was one man who was aware of all this—Samuel Peploe. He had been warden of the Collegiate Church. With the death of Joseph Hoole he determined that this spell should cease so far as St. Ann's was concerned. He appointed Abel Ward.

Mr. Byrom's daughter writes in her diary, "December 28, 1745, Saturday : Mr. Ward was inducted to the rectory of the new church to-day—the bells are ringing for him." On the following day she says, "Sunday, 29 : He (Abel Ward) preached in the afternoon a most furious sermon against Popery. Mr. Lewthwaite (the curate)* and Mr. Johnson drank tea at my uncle's. Mr. Lewthwaite and my mama had a great scolding 'bout these Highlanders ; he abuses them most strangely ; we stayed the evening " (at Kersal Cell). Miss Byrom had again discovered herself to be a strong Jacobite. Private proclivities had increased as personal dangers had decreased. She styles them " rebels " no more. Mr. Lewthwaite appears to have been of a mild and submissive disposition, for he afterwards apologised for his conduct in disagreeing with the elder lady, and seemingly also with Mr. Byrom himself. " December 31, 1745 : Last night Mr. Lewthwaite asked my papa pardon for scolding him."† Evidently the new rector was satisfied with his views, for he remained as curate for six years.

The Rev. Abel Ward was fellow of Queen's College, Cambridge. He took his B.A. in 1740, and proceeded to his master's gown in 1744. In the same year he was collated to a prebendal stall in Chester Cathedral. In the following year the Bishop further added to his favours by presenting him to

* The Rev. Thomas Lewthwaite was probably he who is found as first incumbent of Friarmere, in Saddleworth, in 1768. Canon Parkinson suggests, too, that he was connected with the Lewthwaites of Broad Gate, in Cumberland. Byrom's *Remains*, ii. 386, note.

† This is the last time the curate of St. Ann's is found at the Byrom's. Mr. Ward separated the moth from the candle at once !

the rectorship of St. Ann's. Mr. Ward's preferment was thus somewhat rapid. His strong Georgian sympathies, backed by his great abilities, were doubtless the chief reasons for his advancement. We can readily understand that while the eyes of all England and the Government were fastened upon Manchester, Bishop Peploe, a thorough Whig and Protestant, felt the necessity of promoting a man about whom there could not be the possibility of mistake. In young Ward he had at his hand a man of university distinction, of great natural endowments, and withal as thorough a constitutionalist as himself. The young rector needed all these advantages. For at least four years he had to witness and share in an unceasing war of recrimination. Never such a conflict raged in Manchester as that which followed the downfall of the Pretender, and only finally ceased with the coronation of George the Third.

For two months there had been no rector, and Mrs. Hoole had been at some difficulty to provide a clergyman for the Sunday work. Although several of the Collegiate Church fellows and chaplains had been much compromised by the late rebellion, she was needs obliged to ask Mr. Clayton to help her. Mr. Lewthwaite was not equal to the work alone. Mr. Clayton undertook to take a part of the duty, and as a matter of courtesy he was requested to occupy the pulpit. Miss Byrom, fortunately for the sequence of our narrative, has a word to say about this also. " A paper was read up from the Bishop of Chester to my uncle Edward and Mr. Miles Bower. He called them his 'dearly beloved in Christ'—(evidently the young lady looked upon this as a public declaration of personal affection rather than a mere commonplace of official courtesy)—empowering them to take care of the revenues of the church till such time as he shall put a rector in. Mr. Marriott* and Mr. Joseph

---

* The Marriotts are one of our oldest local families. Joshua Marriott's house may be seen in old prints of Manchester; Marriott's Court still reminds us of the spot. This name is metronymic, being but the old pet

Allen* went out of church because Mr. Clayton preached."
This would cause no little stir ; and no doubt the congregation
would be on the side of the recalcitrants. Mr. Clayton had
prayed openly in the street by Trinity Church, Salford, for
Charles Edward. He had preached in the Collegiate Church
in his behalf. Mr. Allen and Mr. Marriott were the leading
Whigs of the town.

Canon Parkinson, usually so correct in his annotations of
" Byrom's Remains," has fallen into an error in speaking of
Mr. Ward as formerly curate of St. Ann's. 'Tis true that Mr.
Byrom, writing in 1737, says, " I went with Mr. Hoole to
the new church. Mr. Ward read prayers." But this manifestly
could not refer to Abel Ward, as he did not take his degree till

form of Mary. Five or six hundred years ago, Mary was all but unknown
in Lancashire and Yorkshire, *Mariot*, the Norman-French diminutive,
having taken its place in popular favour. All the Manchester Marriotts
for generations were baptized at St. Ann's. Sarah Marriott was married to
Thomas Thackeray in 1798. The Thackerays were a well-established family,
and for several generations acted as stewards to the Mosleys. At this time
they lived at Collyhurst Hall. Two daughters by the above marriage will
always be venerated by the congregation of the late Canon Stowell ; the
elder, married to Joseph Rice, Esq., died in March of the present year.
The present Miss Thackeray is the sole representative of this branch of the
Marriotts. Thackeray, or Thacker, is also a north English name, corres-
ponding to the southern "Thatcher" (compare *dyke* and *ditch, kirk* and
church, poke and *pouch*, etc.). The great novelist sprang from the north,
and from the same stock, I believe. The terminative "y" was common in
old days, hence we find *Vicar* becoming *Vicary*, and *Farmer Farmery*.
The *Manchester Courier*, October 12, 1876, recorded the death of a Mrs.
Farmery.

* The Allens for generations were baptized and buried at St. Ann's.
Mr. Joseph Allen, mentioned in the text, died in 1769, aged seventy years.
His son William, a well-known banker, built Davyhulme Hall. He was
baptized at St. Ann's in 1736, shortly before Mr. Bann's death. His son
Joseph Allen, baptized at St. Ann's December 6, 1770, lived to become
Bishop of Bristol, and died as Bishop of Ely in 1845. A large raised tomb
at the south-east end of the churchyard records the burial of many of this
family.

1740. The fact is Mr. Hoole had a curate at that time of the name of William Ward, possibly a brother of the third rector, as William was a family name. In the burial register occurs, " Thomas, son of the Rev. Mr. Ward, buried Aprill 24, 1740." But there is another entry among the christenings which settles the matter. " William, son of the Rev. William Ward, and Tabetha his wife, was baptized Feb. 23, 1738." *

The Rev. Abel Ward continued rector of St. Ann's for forty years. He was a pluralist to an extent that would be a scandal in the present day, and the history of the church is rather the history of his curates than himself. For about fourteen years he was actively engaged at St. Ann's. During that period his name frequently occurs in the registers, but afterwards more rarely ; and from 1777 to the day of his death (October 1, 1785) his signature is conspicuous by its entire absence. In 1751 he was made Archdeacon of Chester, he being already rural dean of Manchester. The rectory of Dodleston, near the cathedral city, was given to him October 2, 1758. In 1761, only three years later, he became rector of Neston. With three churches on his hands at three corners of the diocese, not to mention his archidiaconal and prebendal duties, we cannot feel surprised to find Mr. Ward vacating the living of Dodleston within four months of his appointment to Neston. As all these preferments were either in the hands of the dean and chapter, or the diocesan, it will be seen that the rector of St. Ann's must have been very popular in high quarters.

Mr. Ward's trumpet gave no uncertain sound ; nay it was a distinct flourish, for he was young and hot. Standing up in the pulpit of St. Ann's, his first discourse was a violent philippic against Popery. Unfettered through his very youth, he heaped

* Query—Was Ormerod's friend Ward, who assisted him in compiling his history of Cheshire, and was so long Diocesan Registrar at Chester, a nephew of Abel Ward ? It is more than likely, since the connection of the Wards with Chester has lasted for 130 years, at least.

up invective upon invective against those who should by any manner of compromise, political or religious, aid and abet that system. The congregation were delighted. Mr. Allen and Mr. Marriott found that they could settle themselves against their high-backed pews in comfort. Mr. Byrom, on the other hand, discovered that St. Ann's was no temple for him to worship in. His reign of patronage was over. No man likes to lose his influence. We can picture the chagrined poet returning to his home, feeling perhaps for the first time in his life, that an intellectual man had come to settle in Manchester, who could dispense with the companionship of the brilliant John Byrom. For once at least the epigrammatist as he wended his way through the square chewed the cud of bitter fancy. It is curious indeed to note the silence on Mr. Byrom's part and that of his daughter as to the affairs of St. Ann's, after the appointment of the new rector, and the delivery of his first sermon. We do not find the worthy gentleman dropping in of an afternoon to see how things were progressing at "the new church." We do not discover that he made an occasional habit of drinking tea with the rector. He is now to be seen dutifully confining himself to the services at the Collegiate Church, close by which his house was situate. He tabooed the very existence of a church over which such a stout champion of the house of Brunswick had come to minister. This silence is very ominous.

And indeed, there was good reason for this. It was but one more defeat where all had been failure. Everything had gone against the Tories and their allies. The year that followed the Pretender's visit was one of continued agitation. Nothing like it had been experienced before. The local magistrates were not idle, and it is just possible they were unnecessarily severe. The disaffected were forced to take oaths of allegiance, the doubtful were harassed, the suspected were watched. Mutual recriminations were heard on every side. The very children fought, and their parents encouraged them. Every little symbol of popular or unpopular sentiment was gloried in. The young Jacobite spark wore his waistcoat in tartan, and affected to be anxious for the Glasgow trade. The school girl, who had worked out the letters "P. C." on her sampler, if challenged, pretended that it meant "Protestant Church" and not "Prince Charlie." Had that modern bit of courtesy been in vogue then, the enquirer might have suggested P. P. C., as they were not likely to see his Royal Highness any more.

The conflict raged with equal vigour in religious circles. So far as they dared the fellows of the Collegiate Church still made their pulpit the vehicle of hostility. If they could not directly thrust at the Government, they could at least make their adversaries the butt of covert attack and open sarcasm. This was met on the part of Mr. Ward and Mr. Nicholls with but more demonstrative loyalty; and I very much fear that had they at this time had a voice in any contemplated revision of the Book of Common Prayer, they would have suggested " Jacobites, Tories, and Nonjurors," as the modern reading for "Jews, Turks, and Infidels." Their church was crowded, not a few of their congregation being Presbyterians, but Presbyterian or Low Churchman, all were alike inflamed with a sense of victory, and filled with a determination to bate no inch of the ground they had won. The Tories had had their triumphs in the past. The hour of Whiggish exultation had come.

Nevertheless the Low Church party had it not all their own way. Rallying from their discomfiture, the High Churchmen came to the fore, and a great paper warfare began. This reached its climax later on, when the riot of October, 1746, gave the adversaries of the Whigs a weapon to fight with. Of course, John Byrom drove his quill. He thus retorts on A. Z., who had defended the action of the Presbyterians :—

"A. Z. presents us kindly with a store
Of three plain truths we never knew before :

And first—the Presbyterians love the Church :
Secondly—King they never left i'th' lurch :
Thirdly—they've no republicans among 'um :
Dingum, Dongum,
Bless us, Old Time ! how our historians wrong 'um."

Another Jacobite, wishing to vent his wrath upon the Whigs, writes a mock censure upon his friends the Fellows. "I shall confine myself, he says, at present to the clergy ; and as in this country place (Manchester), so remote from the centre of wit and politeness, the people are so old-fashioned as to pay great regard to what their teachers say, if I prove them notoriously disaffected, there will need but few arguments to convince the world that the town is itself so. But here I must observe to the reader that I do not intend to cast the least reflection upon our worthy dissenting ministers, and their associates in loyalty, the rector and curates of St. Ann's, who are totally free from every particle of guilt in the following charge."

The sting of this sarcasm was lost. The Cross-street minister, though an estimable man, was now teaching other doctrines than those of Henry Newcombe. 'Tis true the church and the meeting house were mutually sympathetic, but only on national grounds. If a connecting link existed it was forged on a political anvil. If Mr. Mottershead and Mr. Ward's sermons were of a similar cast, it was only that they were speaking as representatives of the loyalty of the community to the reigning house. The 9th October, 1746, was a great day of rejoicing in Manchester. It was the national thanksgiving for the suppression of the rebellion. St. Ann's bell rang from early dawn. The church was crowded from floor to ceiling. Mr. Nicholls preached the sermon. His manner was fervid, and his style was uncompromising. He undertook to prove to an audience already convinced, " that rebels and traitors, guilty of the most atrocious crimes, and whose lives had been as immoral as their deaths were infamous, had no just claims to the distinctions of Christian martyrdom."

Such a discourse was immensely appreciated. It tickled the proclivities of the congregation. The service over, the people poured out, the bells again rang, there was a grand procession of the chief trades of the town—bonfires began to blaze as evening set in—the streets were illuminated—the mob, inflamed with loyalty, and inflated with beer, was ripe for any mischief. Thirty years ago a similar crowd, but of different politics, had wrecked the Presbyterian Meeting House, in Pool Fold. The lurid glare of many lights fell upon the walls of the conventicle. The chapel itself cried out for vengeance. An old score had to be paid off. "Deacon," "Syddall" resounded on every side. In a few minutes the houses of the first primitive bishop and the barber's widow were surrounded, the windows smashed, the doors broken in, and every sign of contumely heaped upon both.

Mr. Nicholls was rewarded—not for the riot, but the discourse—exactly five months afterwards, the king preferring him to the vicarage of Eccles, on the death of Thomas Vaughan. While curate of St. Ann's, he had already been made chaplain to the Earl of Uxbridge. His discourse was so pleasing to the Whig party that it was printed, and circulated among their friends. In the following year he was appointed to preach the assize sermon at Lancaster, in the presence of Sir Thomas Birch.* Its fierce loyalty again commanded admiration, and

---

* Mr. Nicholls's second sermon is entitled, "Obedience to the present Government enforced from the Obligation of our Oaths. A sermon, preached at the Assizes, held at Lancaster by the Honourable Sir Thomas Birch, Knight, and Mr. Baron Legge, on Saturday, September 5th, 1747, by Benjamin Nicholls, A.M., Chaplain to the Right Honourable the Earl of Uxbridge.—Published at the request of the High Sheriff and the gentlemen of the Grand Jury, etc.—London, printed for Henry Whitridge, at the Royal Exchange, mdccxlvii.—Price sixpence." The sermon is dedicated to Samuell Birch, Esq., High Sheriff, and to nineteen other gentlemen, among whom are, Joshua Merriot, Gent., Daniel Bailey, Esq., and Robert Entwistle, Esq.—The text is, "I counsel thee to keep the King's com-

this sermon, too, appeared in print. Another, published in 1753, which was also political, was marked by the same spirit. It was founded on Matthew v. 10 : " Blessed are they that are persecuted for righteousness' sake, for there's *(sic)* is the kingdom of heaven." It is a clever and able discourse, condemning "false cries of persecution." Jacobite and Papist meet no mercy at his hands. Had Mr. Hoole lived a twelvemonth longer, the curate would undoubtedly have been made rector of St. Ann's; but if to be vicar of Eccles was to occupy a less public position, it was to enjoy an ample emolument, and to live at ease, if so be he willed. He died at Eccles, in June, 1765.

The curate was not alone in frank and outspoken utterance. We may conclude this phase of the Church's history by quoting from a published discourse of the rector's. This is the only literary relic I have been able to discover of the archdeacon.* The occasion of its delivery was the anniversary of King Charles' execution. The place was Chester Cathedral. The congregation was a crowd of constitutionalists. The preacher was a young man, of somewhat delicate physique. Few sermons of this period created such a ferment as this. Its ability was only matched by its boldness. Its aim was to

mandment, and that in regard of the oath of God."—Eccles. viii. 2. " A Restriction," " A Duty," " An Inference," are the three heads. He speaks of the nonjuring Pharisees of old, hints that Jacobites teach men to be villains on principle, and raves at Popery, the Pope, and "the Sink of Rome" in a fashion and with a vehemence that would do an Orangeman's heart good.

* The title reads thus: "The Duty of rendering to all their Dues considered. A sermon preached in the Cathedral Church of Chester, on Wednesday, January 30, 1750. By Abel Ward, A.M., Prebendary of Chester. (Manchester: printed by and for R. Whitworth, and sold in London by Mr. Robinson, in Ludgate-street; Mr. Sheepy, under the Royal Exchange; Messrs. Ledsham and Rowley, in Chester; Messrs. Ansdell and Fleetwood, in Liverpool; Mr. Higginson, in Warrington; Mr. Leech, in Knutsford; Mr. Taylor, in Nantwich; and other neighbouring booksellers.) "

set forth the reciprocal duties of prince and people. There can be no doubt that the youthful orator went somewhat further than some of his Whig friends liked, and that in pleasing the Dissenters he made but greater foes of the High Church party. The feeling that the commonalty could make and unmake kings was probably stronger a hundred years ago than now, for then the country could look on such things as acts that had been accomplished within the memory of man. Mr. Ward almost immediately begins, " When a people are found under a limited monarchy as we are (no insignificant, a most valuable blessing, believe it), the same common rule of honesty and mutual benevolence is most verily essential to the tranquillity, to the very existence of the constitution. Each in authority knows wherein lies his power. The very Crown itself is circumscribed, though vested with prerogatives and privileges that are properly its own. And whilst the monarch confines himself within his own legal bounds, and exercises his allotted authority with impartial care and tenderness, he claims, he merits the reverence, the praise, the hearts, the hands of his people. He is as the father, the guardian angel of his country. But should he unhappily, through ambition, or the flattery and persuasion of those about him, invade the rights and liberties of his subjects, the same unfair and forcible measure that he meets to others may, as hath been oft the case, be fatally measured to him again." The prebendary, while treating of Charles the First, was manifestly thinking of James the Second. It was one more blow aimed at his brethren of the Collegiate Foundation—one last shaft let fly at the great doctrine of hereditary and indefeasible right, held in profound reverence by Byrom, Clayton, and the rest. The body of the sermon is then filled in with an "impartial" statement of facts, the object of which was to prove how "a deviation from the rule in the text gave birth to this anniversary." He is hard upon Charles, but it is fair to add that he styles the Opposition party as "a set of miscreants." The execution, if not a martyrdom, was a "murder," committed by "a few ambitious and bloody men."

He concludes with an unquestionable truth. "Again, warn'd sufficiently we are from hence, how *lasting* are the bad effects of national jarrings. They don't expire with the sheathing of the sword, with the noise of the tumult, no, nor with the lives of the multitudes engaged. They are seen for generations, in hatred, in variance, in upbraidings. Even to this day those seeds of contention are not quite rooted out which were scattered abroad somewhat more than one hundred years ago. They are but too visible in the rancour of party rage, and in those intemperate heats and divisions, which to our reproach and sorrow, still occasionally break out amongst us." How true this was Manchester was well aware.

He appeals to his audience not "to lessen legal authority or distress the Government, for that is nothing less than exposing yourselves and party to social harm. And whatever the *sons of rebellion* may insinuate, however restless may be their spirit, and disguised their artifices, lay this up as an undoubted maxim : ' *That no pretence whatever can excuse opposition to Government, but the Governor's proving so unnatural as to attempt its destruction.*'" He then compliments the Sovereign, and concludes : " The more then, inexcusable are we if we refuse to render him filial respect, and all the praise and allegiance due, if, by any means, we knowingly contribute to his uneasiness, or make the diadem he wears a crown of thorns." *

* We may quote a portion of the Preface : " To the Reader. The following sermon was wrote in haste, and of course was never intended for the perusal of the public. Having been attacked, he publishes it. He designed in no degree to justify the unparalleled murder, or to extenuate its guilt . . . . not in truth to do anything more than to point out those stretches of power in King Charles' Government which alarmed and chagrined a free people . . . . As to the studied rude reflections lately vented against the author, most of which, if possible, are as stupid as

Need we say this discourse met with great hostility. It was declared inconsistent with the day commemorated, and inconsistent with itself as an argument. It was at once assailed in the *Chester Courant*, and the Prebendary, strong in his own consciousness of a duty discharged, replied by publishing it as it was delivered. Imagine John Byrom and his daughter entering the church of such a monster of a Whig as this! We can't conceive it, and there is no necessity to try, for we believe they never did.

Abel Ward was rewarded for his outspoken frankness. The archdeaconry of Chester fell vacant. Although the rector of St. Ann's was little more than thirty he was preferred to the office. A year later the bishop himself died, and thus the new archdeacon lost his great patron, friend, and benefactor. He still maintained a close intimacy with the younger Peploe, warden of Christ Church. Father and son had been very much alike in their lives and character. Both were staunch Whigs; both had stood alone as such among the Chapter dignitaries. Both were pious and gentle, and remarkable for their urbanity. An incident in the life of the son may be not without interest. In the *Manchester Mercury*, a paper I shall have to quote frequently by and by, there appeared the following advertisement, June 11, 1754:—"Whereas some months ago, a letter with half-a-crown inclosed was found in the back court of the warden's house, in Manchester, directed to the Reverend Dr. S. Peploe, in Manchester, containing the words following: 'Sir, please to take this half-crown: it was what I once got of your father by a false petition, and I have been

---

they are scurrilous; they are too contemptible to be regarded. If they were calculated to give him uneasiness, they have lost their end; if to harm his reputation, they must, he doubts not, fail in that point . . . . The author leaves such ill-nature and malice to do its own business; the inventors and abettors of such scurrility to be despised as they deserve."—It is remarkable that we have to go to John Byrom's library for so much that his foes wrote and made public.

sorry for it a long time, which makes me take this method to ease myself:' This therefore, is to give notice that if the person who laid, or ordered the letter to be laid there, will make himself known to the said Dr. Peploe, who hereby promises to secrete his name, he shall for his conscientious restitution of a *former* wrong, receive a *present* and generous *reward*." Whether the penitent delinquent came forward we do not know, but the story serves to show that the heart and purse of both bishop and warden were not difficult to reach. The regularity with which the warden attended morning and afternoon prayers made him at those hours of the day as a clock to the towns-people. "True as a needle" his finger pointed to the House of God.

On the 26th February, 1753, just a year after Dr. Peploe's death, Dr. Deacon was buried at St. Ann's, and for all I can find to the contrary, the service was read by Mr. Ward. Such an inconsistency would be remarkable, were it not so easily explained, as we shall show by and by. It is because Dr. Deacon's tomb, raised at the north-east corner of the church-yard, and thus made more prominent than any other grave in Manchester, has helped to give St. Ann's the character of a "famous non-juring church," that we must say a few words about this extraordinary man. No two men in the whole town could be more unlike than these two, Archdeacon Ward and Dr. Thomas Deacon. They were both uncompromisingly resolute, but each in a different cause. Far as the poles asunder were their thoughts and aims. Their churches were near, for Dr. Deacon held forth in an upper room in Fennell-street, but the discourses delivered must have been at conflict indeed. Many of the non-jurors were quite ready to swear to the creeds and the formularies of the English Church, but there the Doctor was even at feud with his own party. He believed in no creed but that he had formulated, would worship in no church but his own, and was firmly convinced there was only one true bishop in Europe—

namely himself. The British Catholic Church—with Dr. Deacon for its diocesan, and its cathedral over the shop in Fennell-street, disagreed with Greek, Roman, and Anglican, on grounds too many for enumeration. Alliance with Dissent was impossible for their lack of episcopacy. All had departed from the primitive Apostolic Church. Dr. Deacon had no less than twelve sacraments—the great two and ten lesser ones, of which anointing with oil, exorcism, the sign of the cross, marriage, holy water, and the wearing of white garments formed a part. His system found a firm defender in one Podmore, a wig-maker.

Thomas Deacon was an ardent adherent of the Stuarts. When the second Pretender's headquarters lay at the Bull's Head, in the Market Place, the Collegiate Church sent its moderate levy of men, but the adjacent "cathedral" was represented by the three sons of the bishop, Thomas Theodorus, Charles Clement, and Robert Renatus (Richard Redemptus was dead), who became officers in the rebel army. As already stated, Thomas Theodorus was executed, and his head placed above the Manchester Exchange.* The bishop gazed with calm resignation, almost with joy, upon the trunkless head of his child, and expressed his thankfulness that he had a son who could thus suffer martyrdom for such a cause. He held firmly by the doctrine of the divine right of kings.

However curious it might seem that Deacon should lie in St. Ann's yard, the explanation is simple. He had for years been at one politically with the Jacobite clergy of the Collegiate Church. They had fought together, if they had not actually coalesced. Shortly, however, before his death, the Doctor had written a work entitled, " Christianity in relation to faith and ritual." He had received the names of all the Tory clergy as subscribers to enable him to print it. Their consternation was great when it was found that the principles expounded therein would seriously

---

* A report is now abroad that his skull was secretly interred in St. Ann's churchyard. (*Vide* Procter's Manchester Streets, p. 266.)

compromise their position to the Church of England. Without being actually Papistical—it was too indefinite for that—the book was certainly not Anglican. The Tory parsons were in a mess. They were accused of abetting the Pope. Another bishop than Deacon, with larger magisterial authority, and uninfected with views about the divine rights, was not likely to pass over the matter lightly. It was with difficulty they righted themselves. One thing, however, was certain. It was next to impossible that Deacon, who died shortly afterwards, should be interred within the collegiate precincts. The clergy of St. Ann's, perfectly free from all complicity, could safely allow burial. The epitaph runs thus: "Here lie interred the remains (which through mortality are at present corrupt, but which shall one day surely be raised again to immortality, and put on incorruption), of Thomas Deacon, the greatest of sinners, and most unworthy of primitive bishops, who died 16th February, 1753, in the 56th year of his age.

Joseph Hoole was buried within forty-eight hours of his death. Ten days elapsed between the death and interment of Thomas Deacon. The one was shuffled as decently as possible into his grave, through fear of public disturbance. The other, through difficulties of a totally different kind, was unable to find a resting place till they that had been his righteous enemies came to his rescue. He was laid to rest in an alien soil, the hopeful promise of his resurrection being uttered by alien lips.

One more matter of political interest, and we have done. Manchester had lit bonfires for the Pretender. Manchester had re-lit them for a rebellion extinguished. It remained to apply the match in behalf of royalty itself. On the 22nd of September, 1761, George the Third was crowned King of England. Nowhere throughout the length and breadth of the land was his coronation so loyally celebrated as in this town. It was the final act of a great local drama. Some few no.

doubt there were who were sore at heart on that day—in secret
they felt the time a bitter one—but the Jacobite spirit was
dying out. Tory and Whig were fast coming to the conclusion
that friendship was a better thing than enmity. Both were
well assured that if the prosperity of the town, so rapidly
grown during the ten years past, was to continue, there
must be a cessation of all hostility. Commerce and common interest were a good basis for union. On that day
they buried their feuds in the bowl that was pledged to King
George. There was, of course, a service at St. Ann's in the
morning. Who preached the sermon, I cannot say; but
though Mr. Ward was now snugly esconced as rector of
Neston, we may well believe he would not be unwilling to
catch the Chester "Highflyer," and take his part in the
festivities of the day. No doubt he discoursed to his
parishioners in right loyal style. On this occasion, we may
suppose, he rather dwelt on a present that promised so much
blessing to the country, than a past which was embittered
with troubles of which he had had something to do. Out of
church the congregation, with the rest of the townspeople, gave
themselves up to pleasure. From a stage in St. Ann's Square
barrels of beer and casks of wine were emptied at the king's
expense. License to be drunk on the premises would, I fear,
be the order of that day. Doubtless, too, among the seven
hundred ladies and gentlemen who attended the final ball in
the Exchange assembly rooms on the following night, would be
found many a pew-owner of Constitutional St. Ann's. *

Thus ends the political phase of St. Ann's history. Henceforth her life flows on a slower and calmer tide. The ship has
reached safe waters. It is hard to picture, as we gaze on her

---

* The Manchester paper describing this ball says, "In an apartment
contiguous a very grand collection of fruits, sweetmeats, and confectionaries
of all sorts was disposed (not disposed of) in a very elegant manner."
Thus was a supper described a century ago.

quiet sanctuary, and still more quiet resting place for the sleeping dead, that strife has here been high. As when we look upon the placid, unruffled sweetness of some aged woman's face, it is hard to believe that passion has ever been at war there, and not till we have scanned her secret diary, yellow with time, and blotched with tears, can we find a record of days when the conflict of life raged strong and bitterly, so hard is it to believe that faction has made here its battle ground, and not till we have looked more narrowly upon those time-worn archives that reveal her past, can we estimate the struggles through which she has been called to pass.

Henceforward the Church of St. Ann's rides in the safe bay of parochial interest. Its tide is sluggish, but its perils are few. Here also we must practically close the career of Archdeacon Ward. He continued to be rector of St. Ann's for a quarter of a century after this, but the church and parish saw little of him. It was not merely that he held several other offices of greater or less importance which required his presence. We gather from several allusions in the local prints that he was of feeble constitution. A man of brilliant faculties, he lacked physical power. The remainder of his life was passed in attending to that part of his many duties which lay betwixt Chester and Neston. Of his death, and the manner of his death, we shall speak in our next chapter. Here however, ends his connection with Manchester. This at least can be said of him, that he did not leave the town till he had performed the work allotted to him when Samuel Peploe sent him there. He bravely upheld the Constitution as it existed, and as boldly controverted the now all but obsolete doctrine of the hereditary indefeasible right of kings. But he was no time-server. No man in the last century, throughout the length and breadth of England, was more bold than Abel Ward to remind his monarch that he who sits upon the British Throne, sits there on conditions, and that the duties of king and subject are of a reciprocal character.

V.

ABEL WARD'S CURATES.

S already stated, Abel Ward was preferred to the Archdeaconry of Chester in 1751. It was the last of many favours heaped upon him by his attached friend, Samuel Peploe. The discharge of his new duties took him frequently to the Cathedral City, and the rectory of Dodleston, as afterwards that of Neston, was much more accessible and conveniently placed than a rented house in King-street, or Ridgefield. It was only natural, too, that, with his enfeebled health, he should decide to live in the more bracing and wholesome atmosphere of a Cheshire village. Pluralities, now a recognised evil, and one the removal of which has occupied, and successfully occupied, the attention of Churchmen, were a hundred years ago rather the rule than the exception. Probably, it never occurred to the Archdeacon's mind that a resident shepherd is better than an hireling. The first stage towards the removal of an ingrained disease is to be aware of its presence. Abel Ward, and hundreds of other beneficed clergymen, were as yet unconscious of an evil which, like a canker, was eating away the very energy and life of the Church. If the Church's pulse was beating slow a century ago, we must lay much of its languor to the door of the pluralist.

We can readily understand that it was a matter of importance to secure as coadjutors at St. Ann's—or, to speak more
strictly, curates in charge—men of experience and discretion.
The archdeacon was happy in his selections. Of Benjamin
Nicholls we say nothing. We have already described him.
Besides he was Joseph Hoole's appointment, and did not long
stay with his successor. From 1751 to the day of Mr. Ward's
death in 1785, the nominal rectorship of St. Ann's was held by
two men ; for the first twenty-six years by the Rev. Humphrey
Owen ; for the remaining eight years by the Rev. Samuel
Hall. Mr. Owen was in reality chaplain of the Collegiate
Church. Under some arrangement of which we do not
now know all the particulars, he took the daily prayers and
other surplice work at St. Ann's, and at such seasons as were
agreed upon between the archdeacon and the Chapter, was res-
ponsible for the Sundays also. In this position he was assisted
by a regular curate, the first being a Rev. Mr. Reed (1751-2),
the second a Rev. Mr. Griffiths, who seems to have stayed,
like Mr. Lewthwaite, more than six years at least. Even at
this early period Mr. Ward could not have frequented his
parish often, for if we consult the occasional advertisements of
Harrop's newspaper, we shall find that Mr. Owen was on
all greater festivals the alone preacher.

Humphrey Owen was born at Aberystwith, being himself of
Welsh descent, in 1723, and took his degree at St. John's College,
Oxford. He was attached to Christ Church as chaplain after
he had been in orders a short time—and for twenty-six years
laboured assiduously in the parishes of the two central churches.
He came at a critical time. The building of St. Mary's in 1756
could not but have its effect upon St. Ann's. To the curate it
was at once an advantage and a drawback, for while it took a
large share of his work, the new church was considered one
of the handsomest of the time, and was quickly filled with
a fashionable congregation, not a few being old pew-owners

of St. Ann's. The Parsonage and the Parade were occupied by well-to-do residents. The west-end people of Gartside-street and upper Deansgate had but to follow the street to reach the new church. Sedan chairs had a straight course, and were less liable to be jostled. St. Mary's began well.

Nevertheless St. Ann's flourished with but little dimmed splendour. Some of the best families the neighbourhood could boast were to be found there. Sir John Parker Mosley, the great man of the town, was an habitual attendant. Joshua Marriott's children and grandchildren, a little congregation of themselves, worshipped there. The Allens, the Sedgwicks, the Entwistles, the Philips, the Bartons (now of Stapleton Park), the Pattens, or at least Jonathan Patten, from whose elder brother are descended the Wilson-Pattens—now represented by a member of the Upper House—all these steadily adhered to the church, in which most of them had been baptised by Bann or Hoole, and whose children were being baptised by Owen or Griffiths. Many a fustian manufacturer, fast growing rich, had his pew there. A little later on leading surgeons, like Alexander Eason, of Lever's Row, Richard and Edward Hall, father and son, of Deansgate, and Micah Ward, of King-street—conspicuous attorneys, like Oswald Milne and Joseph Chippendale—prominent wine merchants, or "liquor merchants," as they were at that time styled, like Joseph Armstrong and James Clough—and Miles Bower, the great hatter,* were among Humphrey Owen's auditors. Mr. Joseph

---

* Miles Bower was buried at St. Ann's in 1780, aged 84. His son John, baptised at St. Ann's, April 5, 1747, married the heiress, Miss Jodrell, and took her name. Jodrell-street by Gartside-street, close to the spot where Miles lived, commemorates the connection thus formed. John Bower Jodrell died at Bath in 1796. The Taxall estate, near Whaley-bridge, came to him through Foster Bower, one of the first legal men of his day. Dying in 1785, he bequeathed the property to his brother. Foster Bower was baptised at St. Ann's, May 30, 1748. The name of "Bower" still remains on one of the pews in the middle aisle.

Armstrong took the first house in the new street, called, I believe, after the Princess Augusta, and for a century his descendants kept the same premises till driven into King-street by the "City" Hall of 1876. We must not forget, too, Henry Worrall, the most popular citizen of his day, who acted as chairman at the Exchange Coffee Rooms when the manufacturers met to obtain a repeal of the obnoxious Fustian Act. The names of nearly all these gentlemen still remain on the brass labels of the pew doors.

Few of these had far to come. They lived in the parish— in King-street, St. Ann's Square, Ridgefield, or St. James's Square. Market-street, too, sent its foremost shopkeepers, who of course lived on their premises. Daniel Lynch, chemist, had a pew at St. Ann's 100 years ago. Newton, the bookseller, Ravald, the coffee-house keeper, Rose and Howard, the grocers, came from the same neighbourhood.*

In 1789 the church of St. Michael, in Angel Meadow, was consecrated. Mr. Owen, I believe, was the chief instrument of its erection, and as being such, received the first appointment. It was arranged that he and his family should have the presentation for sixty years, after which the right was to go into the hands of the warden and fellows. The new rector did not long enjoy his changed position, for he died in November, 1790. His tomb and tablet may be seen at the Collegiate Church.

Mr. Owen had married Miss Mary Nicholls, whether a relation of Benjamin Nicholls or not, I cannot say. By her he had a family, as St. Ann's register can show. His son John Owen,

---

* Poor John Howard's friends gave him an unfortunate epitaph, one, too, that reflected unkindly upon his wife. It may still be seen in the churchyard.—"Here lyeth the body of John Howard, who died Jan. 2, 1800, aged 84 years; 50 years a respectable grocer, and a honest man." As it is further stated that his wife died in 1749, fifty years before, it would seem her husband's honesty dated from the day of her decease. Mrs. Malaprop herself in her happiest moments could not have beaten this inscription.

of Manchester, attorney at law, baptised at St. Ann's, Sept. 8, 1759, was buried at the Collegiate Church in 1831, aged seventy-two. He lived for many years at 29, Gartside-street, during the time when that street was a fashionable suburb. He had been educated at the Manchester Grammar School, and I think Mr. Smith or Mr. Hibbert-Ware has a story of his constant attendance at the School Feast, at which he would sing with the Earl of Wilton, even to the day when extreme age had made his voice thin and shrill.

But "revenons à nos moutons." On the retirement of Humphrey Owen in 1777, he was succeeded by the Rev. Samuel Hall, M.A., one of the best known men of his day. Mr. Hall came from a family that had dwelt for generations in the immediate neighbourhood of Ashton.* Educated at the school of that town he took his degree at Catharine Hall, Cambridge, being placed fifth among the Senior Optimes. As curate in charge of St. Ann's Mr. Hall had, unlike his predecessor, no connection with Christ Church. That his labours should be confined wholly to the parish was absolutely necessary. The population had vastly increased, and the rector had finally given up even the semblance of work there. The Archdeacon may have visited the church after the appointment of his new *locum tenens*, but there is no proof of it, and from his enfeebled state it is probable that he never did so. Every advertisement of charity and other sermons announces Mr. Hall as preacher. In May, 1776, a year before he entered upon his labours, the curate married Elizabeth Russell at the Collegiate Church. She was daughter of the Rev. Radclyffe Russell, vicar of Easingwold, Yorkshire.† Her father lies in Prestwich church-

* Mr. Hall preached the first Sunday-school anniversary sermon in Ashton parish church, in 1784.

† Her mother seems to have been buried at St. Ann's. "Mary, wife of Rev. Mr. Russell, May 16th, 1738."—Register. The Russells had a house in Manchester, for in 1771, Mr. Russell himself is stated in the *Mercury* to have died "at his house in Manchester, March 21st."

yard. His connection with that place arose from his marrying the daughter of the Rev. Jacob Scholes, whose name will be still familiar to some, the tradition of his sixty-one years' ministry as curate of Prestwich not being likely to die out.* The old veteran's grand-daughter, Mr. Hall's wife, was baptised at St. Ann's in 1751, and died at Cheadle in 1815. Eleven children are registered as baptised at the church of which her husband was curate, between 1777 and 1791; most of them died young, and are buried in the churchyard.

To Mr. Hall belongs the honour of having preached the first Sunday-school anniversary sermon at St. Ann's. The *Manchester Mercury* for October 18, 1785, thus alludes to that event: "Sunday last a sermon was preached at St. Ann's Church, by the Rev. Samuel Hall,† for the benefit of those humane institutions the Sunday-schools, from these words : 'To do good and to distribute, forget not.' The children sung some particular hymns selected for the occasion, and a very handsome collection was made for the further support of that noble charity." We shall say more upon this subject in our succeeding chapter.

It must not be supposed that Mr. Hall's influence was confined to the boundaries of St. Ann's parish. Possessed of great versatility, he was alike welcome in social and literary circles. Of the latter, he was for twenty years the ruling spirit. The Manchester Literary and Philosophical Society was founded in 1781, chiefly through Mr. Hall's exertions, and in

---

* In 1747, the ages of the different functionaries at Prestwich were as follows:—Richard Goodwin, Rector, 70; Jacob Scholes, curate, 78; Ralph Guest, churchwarden, 85; Richard Diggle, clerk, 85; Ann Diggle, his wife, 78; Edmund Berry, sexton, 76; Mary Berry, his wife, 86; total, 588 years, giving to each something over 79 years.

† Ten years earlier, the Rev. Samuel Hall would have been described as the "Rev. Mr. Hall." Just now it was becoming the fashion to drop the Mr. and insert the Christian name. This mode of address still prevails.

1784 we find him occupying the position of vice-president.*
Our Mechanics' Institutions are not one of the least important
results of the origination of this body.   As the reader walks
towards the pulpit of St. Ann's, up the centre aisle, he may
still see the "Rev. Samuel Hall, 1784," inscribed upon a brass
label above one of the pew doors.   There his family worshipped, while he led the services.   It has never been removed,
and remains as a self-placed but modest memento of his labours
as practical rector of St. Ann's.   On the appointment of Mr.
Sandford, the junior curate, he still continued his connection
with the church.   In 1794, however, he was made rector of
the new church called St. Peter's, at the bottom of the street
whose name commemorates the Mosley family.   A portion of the
scene of his past ministry was taken to form the new parish, and
thus from his ordination to his death, he continued in a sense
to hold office among the same people, and in the same sphere.

* The curate of St. Ann's had a clever family. John Hall, born October
9th, 1785, apprenticed in 1803 to Dr. Ward, one of the surgeons to Manchester
Infirmary, elected M.R.C.S. in 1810, settled at Congleton 1814, and died
November 27th, 1861, aged 76, much respected. He left a daughter and
three sons, the eldest of whom, Charles Radcliffe Hall, M.D., resides at
Torquay. His daughter, Francis Russell, married John Wyatt, Esq., of
Congleton. His other sons John Fielden Hall, J.P., and George William
Hall, are resident in that town.—(*Vide* Mr. Smith's Gram. Sch. Reg.)–Francis
Russell Hall, born 17th May, 1788, graduated at St. John's, Cambridge,
being placed tenth wrangler in 1810. Became fellow, A.M., 1813, B.D.
1820, D.D. 1839, rector of Fulbourne, near Cambridge, 1826, and died
November 18th, 1866, aged 78, leaving a daughter and three sons. He
published several small works: "Hints to Young Clergymen," 1843,
reached a third edition.—(*Vide* Gram. Sch. Reg.)—Samuel Hall, eldest son,
held a Manchester Exhibition at St. John's, Cambridge, B.A. 1804, seventh
Sen. Opt., fellow on Platt Foundation, M.A., 1807. He took orders,
became curate to his father at St. Peter's, then perpetual curate of Billinge,
in the parish of Wigan. He resigned this after his adoption of universalist
views, believing that no one could possibly perish. He had been an extreme
Calvinist. He died in London, 1858, 21st October, leaving three sons and
two daughters. (*Vide* Gram. Sch. Reg.)

It may seem strange that Mr. Hall should be passed over by the bishop, when the archdeacon died, and his junior appointed. This may be explained by the fact that it was generally known that Mr. Hall was to be elected a fellow of the Collegiate Church when a vacancy occurred. St. Ann's was the only church in the Manchester parish in the gift of the bishop. The new churches that were springing up were all to be vested in the hands of the Collegiate Chapter after two appointments made by the family of the founder. Holders of fellowships were constantly preferred to these churches; but never to St. Ann's, although I am not aware that the diocesan was legally incapacitated from making such an appointment. This, however, is the reason why St. Ann's, during the present century at least, has become so completely dissociated, in a sense, from its mother church. The Chapters have preferred their own men to the other town churches; the Bishop of Chester alone has appointed his man to St. Ann's. This difference has had some slight effect upon the two oldest churches in their mutual relations. I do not find that there has been much interchange of pulpits during the last hundred years. There has ever been an interchange of cordial courtesies, but nothing more. Jealousy has had nothing to do with this, nor even Jew and Samaritan tendencies. It is the natural result of two churches standing close beside one another, the younger of which is wholly unfettered from the older. It is—or I should say has been—a kind of unconscious antagonism.

The story of Mr. Hall's appointment to St. Peter's is interesting. It will be found in Canon Wray's "Memoirs." It appears that the curate of St. Ann's was chaplain to the local volunteers, several gallant companies having been raised during the American War. At one of the special services held in the church, Mr. Hall, not wishing to hurt the consciences of the Presbyterian and other Dissenting members of the corps,

omitted the Athanasian Creed.*   At this very time there fell a
vacancy among the fellows of Christ Church.   It was generally
understood that the chaplain to the volunteers was to fill it.
But the chapter was alike alarmed and offended, and to quote
the late venerable and still venerated canon's words, " he lost
his election by deferring to the prejudices of his audience,
instead of performing his duties as prescribed by the Church."
But this in turn offended Mr. Hall's friends, and he had many.
To make up for his disappointment, for he had lost both St.
Ann's and the Fellowship, they rallied about him, added largely
to the subscriptions for the proposed church at the foot of the
new and already most fashionable street of the town, and thus
procured for him the preferment as first rector.

We have spoken incidentally of St. Mary's, St. Michael's
and St. Peter's.   It is fitting that we should mark the great
change that was passing over the town.   It will again remind
us how distinctly the building of churches gauges the progress
of industry, and consequently the increase of population.   The
forty years of Archdeacon Ward's life, as rector of St. Ann's,
is commercially the most important era in the career of the
town.   Manchester's position in the world was decided.   It
saw a most rapid growth of population, and, as a consequence,
of religious activity.   Defoe, already quoted, writing in 1727,
speaks of a " new church," other than St. Ann's, as being pro-
jected.   It is somewhat curious to note that this third sanctuary
was not erected until thirty years after this statement was published.   The cause is not far to seek.   The import of cotton
had received a severe check for many years.   In 1701 the
quantity of cotton wool imported into England was 1,985,868
lbs. ; in 1730 it had fallen to 1,545,472.   In 1701 the official

* There can be little doubt that Mr. Hall was an extremely broad
Churchman for his day. Dr. Barnes, of Cross-street Chapel, was on the
closest terms of intimacy with him. I strongly suspect the curate was not
unwilling to omit the creed in question.

value of British cotton goods (so-called) exported of all sorts was £23,253 ; in 1730 this estimate had fallen to £13,524.*

One chief source of this deterioration was our commercial legislation. That we must look here for the cause is the more palpable, inasmuch as this is the period of the great thirty years' quietude that succeeded the Peace of Utrecht, 1714. The woollen manufacture, our great staple industry, had become jealous of its new rival. It attacked the import of Indian cotton goods. In 1700 an Act passed prohibiting the import of printed and dyed calicoes of India, Persia, and China. This failing of its intent, a further Act was passed in 1721, imposing a penalty of £5 on all folk found wearing printed or stained calico, whether made at home or abroad. With this stringent enactment the import of cotton wool into England seems to have begun again to decline.† Not till 1736 did the "Manchester Act" pass which relieved the town from its depressed state. In 1764, the year of Kay's fly-shuttle, and Hargreaves's spinning-jenny, the import of cotton wool was 3,870,382 lbs., the value of its exported goods being £200,354. After this its progress, with occasional drawbacks and hindrances, was rapid.

The growth of population being thus retarded for so many years, the need of church accommodation did not present itself so strongly, and it was not till 1756 that the church contemplated in 1727 was consecrated. It was called St. Mary, probably owing to the tradition that the Saxon church of that name stood in the immediate neighbourhood. It is curious to trace the connection between inland navigation and the site upon which this church was built. So early as 1720 an act had been passed permitting the inhabitants of Liverpool and Manchester to deepen the channel of the rivers Mersey and Irwell. In process of time, and notably by the middle of the

---

* *Vide* Baines's "Cotton Manufacture," quoted by Espinasse.
† Espinasse, "Lancashire Worthies," p. 298.

H

last century, when the great cutting was made above Warrington, which not merely shortened but made much safer the course, the intercommunication was mightily improved between the two great towns. This, as a matter of consequence, led to a great increase of population along the Irwell bank upon the Manchester side from Blackfriars to Quay-street. St. Mary's is but a memorial of this. Nevertheless, although built for the wants of a lower class, St. Mary's was for a period the fashionable church of the town. It was considered to have the handsomest spire in Lancashire. The wealth and influence of its congregation could nearly swamp both the Old Church and St. Ann's together. But it had to succumb. It has laboured for years under a disadvantage peculiarly its own. It is so built up that, although in the centre of the town, hundreds of Deansgate wayfarers are unaware of its existence. It is like a still pool fast beside a swift current. The tide of human life and passion sweeps swiftly by, and yet itself is wholly untouched. It still struggles bravely under the present rector, Dr. Beddoes. St. Mary's was built much too nearly to St. Ann's. But our forefathers were no more gifted with prescience than ourselves, and they could not possibly have contemplated the present position of the centre of Manchester. Meadowland still stretched away beyond the Quay-street, and across the river was a wide expanse of rurality. The first rector, the Rev. John Gatley, died soon after his appointment, and he was succeeded by the Rev. Thomas Foxley, who also enjoyed but a short tenure, for he died October 17, 1761. Both were fellows of the Collegiate Church.

The tide of population then turned Shudehill way, and filled the interstices betwixt High-street and the Collegiate Church. A new church dedicated to St. Paul, and called St. Paul's Chapel, was there built, and consecrated July 28, 1765. But this was not enough. Both Kay's and Hargreaves' inventions were in full play. Gardens made place for dwelling-houses ;

fields began to disappear before a compact and still encroaching army of tenements; and within three years a church was again needed in the direction of Deansgate, this time rather for the better class of people. In fact it was to be the great suburban church on the Chester Road. The utmost respectability prevailed in Byrom-street, Gartside-street, and the upper part of Quay-street. Indeed, these thoroughfares bade fair to throw the solemn seclusion of King-street and Ridgefield into the shade. Edward Byrom, son of John Byrom, laid the first stone of St. John's, so called after his father, April 28, 1768, and it was consecrated June 7, 1769. The Rev. John Clowes (whose father, Joseph Clowes, had been wont to worship at St. Ann's) and the Rev. William Huntington held the rectorship for 105 years, a fact, I was almost about to say a feat, unprecedented. As in the case of the other churches, a special act provided that the founder's family should have the first and second presentation—after that the collegiate chapter. This privilege did not become theirs until the year 1874, when the present rector, Mr. Henn, well known in his relationship to the Hospital Sunday movement, received the appointment.

Piccadilly, and the neighbourhood of Upper Mosley-street, required a church next; and in 1786 Dr. Cornelius Bayley laid the foundation stone of St. James', in George-street, one more title commemorative of the reigning family. This sanctuary was consecrated August 18th, 1788. This year was a remarkable one in our church annals. The population of Manchester and Salford had increased to over 50,000 souls. The need of an especial effort to meet this rapid growth was strongly felt. The foundation of St. Peter's Church was laid December 11th; that of St. Michael's, Angel Meadow, May 20th; while the month of August saw St. James' ready for public worship. Dr. Cornelius Bayley was a well-known man in his day, not to say his wife, who could be recognised from the top to the bottom of Market-street by her Amazonian proportions. The

worthy doctor was son of a leather-breeches seller in the neighbourhood of High-street. This in posting days was a most
important occupation, and no wonder the father made a small
fortune out of it. Cornelius was thus enabled to go to college,
but a difficulty arose at the time of his ordination, he being so
extremely Jewish in appearance that his bishop hesitated to
proceed in the office. Cornelius settled it by proposing to eat
pork at the episcopal dinner, especially if his lordship would see
that the onions were properly done. Another story, handed
down by tradition, is that when he returned from the university
with his doctor's hood, he found himself caricatured in Manchester as wearing a pair of leather breeches, each leg grace-
fully coming over the shoulders, and pinned in front.* Dr.
Bayley is reported to be the founder of Sunday-schools in Manchester, but, as will appear in our next chapter, this primary
honour seems far from being his. St. James' robbed St.
Mary's of the title of being the fashionable church, but this
act of piracy was short-lived. In 1794 the new Doric structure,
with Whyatt for its architect, and dedicated to St. Peter, was
completed. It became at once the shrine to which the "fashionable sinners" of Mosley-street and Piccadilly turned their steps
one day in seven. Even Dr. Law, the Bishop of Chester,
could not forbear an episcopal sneer at the character of its
worshippers. Down to the days of Dr. Jeremiah Smith, the
musical performances (if one may use such a lay expression),
and greater attempt at refinement in the services, made St.
Peter's the haunt of all the frequenters of the "Assembly
Rooms," and fashionable idlers of the town. It was " a place
of resort" rather than a temple of worship.† Let not the

* I see Mr. Harland recounts both these stories in his "Manchester
Collectanea." I first received them by oral tradition.

† I need not say that under the careful hands and skilled knowledge of
Dr. Joule, the music at St. Peter's will still bear comparison with that of
any church in Lancashire. That the congregation are not now "fashionable idlers" requires no refutation.

reader mistake. For years after this St. Peter's faced on its southern side nought but fields and a few farmsteads; and there was ample room in 1819 in "St. Peter's fields" for that meeting of over 60,000 people, which was dispersed by the yeoman cavalry at a cost of eight lives. There are many still living who can describe the place as well as the sensation of Peterloo. We may note in passing that the Friends' Meeting House in Mount-street was built in 1795; St. Mary's Catholic Chapel in Mulberry-street in 1794; and the New Jerusalem Church, Peter-street, in 1793. Many of Mr. Clowes' congregation from St. John's worshipped in the latter, his views tending much to mysticism. Thus it will be seen that the religious activity of the last decade of the 18th century in Manchester was great, and far from being confined to one body. This is probably the quietest, we might almost add the dullest, period of St. Ann's history. Looking at the records of this date, we should be almost inclined to say that the building of so many churches had somewhat damped its spirit, as it had unquestionably crippled its influences.

Mr. Hall had an ardent co-adjutor in his clerk, James Kay. Were we at all superstitious we should be inclined to fear his ghost rising before our eyes—and we are writing this at the witching hour of night—rebuking us for our delay in bringing his august presence before the public. At once we begin: "James Kay" appears on a pew door in the north gallery, the date being 1780. That such small fry as the Oldfields, the Bagshaws, the Philips, and the Bowers should have brass labelled doors, and not the Kays, as represented by himself, was out of the question. James Kay, I repeat the twofold name, for oft he must have repeated it with pride to himself, was clerk of St. Ann's. And of all the clerks wont to speak of, "I and the rector," he must have been first. To Mr. Kay we owe the double list of rectors and clerks given up to this date in the smaller register book. It is in his own handwriting. On the *first* page is the list of clerks, appended to which is

" memorandum by J. Kay." On the *second* page is a list of the rectors, again " memorandum by J. Kay," being set at the top. In a Manchester directory for 1794, I find he is thus registered : " James Kay, tailor, habit-maker, and robe-maker, and clerk of St. Ann's Church, 14, St. Ann's Alley." Evidently he could give you the lay, clerical, and even lady equestrian cut, at your will, and according to the fashion prevailing in the highest society. To the poorer classes, I fear, he gave the cut direct. He was clerk from 1775 to 1810, nearly thirty-five years, and doubtless grew more consequential as he grew more patriarchal. Wherever there is a chance of setting down his name, his quill is in the ink-pot. Unfortunately for a man of his lofty position his education had been neglected. He could spell his own name correctly, but no one else's.* The Pickerings are set down as " Pikrins," Sybil becomes " Sibble," and in the same plastic hands, Pamela (in much requisition at the font just now) is easily transformed into " Permealea." He heads a page with the information that these are the " Christenings at St. Ann's in 1799." But having subverted the order of several, he adds an explanatory note to the effect that they have been " rong placed." These are but a few examples of the clerkly amenities of James Kay. He must have thoroughly enjoyed his office, in spite of his ignorance of the original sense of the term " clerk." It must have been a matter of genuine satisfaction to him when the new hymn book was published—his name was in it, and in print. The book is entitled, "Select Portions of Dr. Brady's and Mr. Tate's Version of the Psalms ; together with a few selected from the old version. Also a Collection of Hymns and Sanctuses† for the use of

---

* Archdeacon Kaye once told my father that his name had this peculiarity. You might spell it with four, three, two, or even one letter, and it remained Kaye. (Kaye, Kay, Ka, K.)

† There seems to have been a professional choir. We are informed that an anthem will be sung on Sunday next in St. Ann's Church, in the afternoon, for the benefit of the singing boys.—*Harrop's Mercury*, March 29th, 1785.

St. Ann's Church, Manchester. 'Let the word of Christ dwell in you richly in all wisdom; teaching and admonishing one another in psalms and hymns and spiritual songs; singing with grace in your hearts to the Lord.' To be had of J. Kay, clerk, only. Manchester: Printed by C. Wheeler, 1784."* This compilation would doubtless be Mr. Hall's work. The rector was too old and infirm for such a task. Such a surmise is confirmed by the preface to the hymns and sanctuses. The curate in charge as a leading literary spirit of his day would not be sorry to subjoin Milton's lines—

> Now let the pealing organ blow,
> To the full-voic'd choir below,
> In service high, and anthems clear,
> As may, with sweetness through mine ear,
> Dissolve me into extacies,
> And bring all heaven before mine eyes.

Byrom's new hymn, "Christians awake," is of course found therein.†

* I am indebted for a copy of this book to Richard Wood, Esq., formerly churchwarden of St. Ann's. Mr. Wood is one of the first antiquarians in Manchester. It is a public loss that through diffidence or reticence he should keep his acquired knowledge to himself.

† A curious note at the end of the compilation declares that "this book contains all the hymns used at St. John's Church, and St. Paul's Chapel, Manchester, and St. Thomas's Chapel, Ardwick, and by observing the following direction, will be found equally useful at any of the above places of worship. For example, if the 7th hymn is wanted at St. John's, look in the first column of the numbers belonging to that church for 7, and over against it is 43, which is the 43rd hymn in this book. Again, if the 7th hymn is wanted at St. Paul's, look in the first column of the numbers, and over against it is 5, which is the 5th psalm in this book; and so for all the rest." Thus we see that, although each church had its separate hymn-book, they were all published in concert. The explanatory note did not apply, however, to St. Thomas's. An additional clause says, "the numbers stand the same in the Ardwick book as in St. Ann's."

It only remains to be added that James Kay died in 1810, and was buried within a yard of his door-step. He was succeeded in the clerkship by Mr. Brookes, who for twenty years at least was one of the leading musical spirits of the town. The glee clubs of Manchester would have fared ill without his services. He lived at Swinton, and I believe is buried there.

What extraordinary changes had taken place in the parish and town during the clerical tenancy of Owen and Hall. They had seen Manchester with but two churches, the Collegiate fabric and their own. Year after year one church had been added to another; and now let them turn to any point of the compass, and a spire or tower stood out against the sky. They had seen fields and gardens within the limits of their own sphere of work covered with tenements, and, as they cast their eye beyond their parish bounds, some slight conception of future Manchester must have dawned upon their wandering vision. They could already point to poor men waxen rich, and men of moderate fortunes grown opulent, through the manufacture of fustians. Nor was it increase alone they saw. Already the work of demolition had beome necessary. A prospering community must uproot as well as plant. Both lived in the most eventful year of Manchester's structural life, 1776. Just one hundred years ago it was, when the centre of Manchester for the first time saw the primary blow struck at its ancient aspect. Manchester became a new town then. St. Mary's Gate, Cateaton-street, and Old Millgate, as our forefathers knew them, disappeared. So narrow were they that an overloaded vehicle could not pass. They were mere passages. Down came quaint gables that hung over the pathway, down came strange devices of lath and plaster, down came all that was picturesque and prettily irregular. Exchange-street fared similarly. The cobbler's stall disappeared from the "dangerous corner;" the pump from the "dark entry." No more could the peruke come in contact with the ceiling as the exquisite climbed the narrow staircase to gossip over a cup of coffee in Ravald's rooms. Whipp the saddler had to saddle horses elsewhere; and Newton—he lies in St. Ann's Churchyard—had notice to quit, for Acres Court was to come down.

One of the greatest changes Mr. Owen beheld, when he vacated his post, was the abolition of sign-boards in Market-street Lane. In December, 1771, a notice was issued to this effect : " With the approbation and concurrence of the magistrates, we, the boroughreeve and constables request the shopkeepers and innholders of this town, who have not already taken down their signs, to do the same as soon as possible, and place them against the walls of their houses, as they have been long and justly complained of as nuisances. They obstruct the free passage of the air, annoy the passengers in wet weather, darken the streets, etc., all which inconvenience will be prevented by a compliance with our request, and be manifestly productive both of elegance and utility. Thomas Scott, Benjamin Bower, John Bell." The natural result of this request was the entire removal, in most cases, of the obnoxious signboards, and the adoption of numbered houses. Manchester, I believe, was the first town in the country, after London, to fall upon this device. A directory, published in 1772, by Elizabeth Ravald, who obtained a national renown by her book on cookery, describes Mr. Owen as living at the " top of Deansgate." This was the last year of unnumbered doors. Mr. Byrom, writing to his wife from Cambridge or London, had always to address his letters to " Mrs. Byrom, near the old church, in Manchester." In 1773 the directory furnishes numbers after the name.* This was a great advance. It is from this time we note the gradual diminution of posters and swinging sign-boards. Anyone looking at one of the old

* London had adopted the plan only three years earlier. In the preface to " Kent's Directory for 1770," he states that the doors are now first numbered " in accordance with the late Act of Parliament."

pictures of our streets will observe the extent to which these were employed to give individuality to the shopkeeper. While four-fifths of the people could not read, a name and a number were useless. Every shop had its sign : " The Lamb," the "Three Crowns," the "Red Lion," the "Blue Boar," the "Bull," or the " Hart." Inns, hostelries, and public-houses have still retained these ensigns. In 1772 Mr. Owen is " at the top of Deansgate." In 1773 he has a numbered address. We cannot conceive ourselves in 1876 without these marks of local identification. Yet as an institution they are but a century old.

But a few months after the removal of Acres Court, and the " Old Bridge," too, was only a memory. There, too, commerce, with its hundred exigencies, demanded more space. The dungeon must be taken away, the piers and arches extended, and the old folks are shaking their heads. No more will they see the pedestrian dodging into the angular recesses till the steaming coach has rumbled by. No more will the prisoner hear the water flowing fast beside his confined cell, and as he notes the dripping rain and rising flood, begin to wish his mother had given him a caul, and wonders whether it be really true that he who is born to be hanged shall never be drowned. I wonder could he watch from grated window the nimble trout, or catch the distant glimpse of some sober citizen rambling through Strangeways meadows, to sniff the wholesome air under Kersal Brow. We may presume the river was still pure. Mr. Berry in his map, not twenty years earlier, says : " The river Irwell washes a great part of the town." Our objection now is that while it still performs its time-honoured office, it does not wash the city quite so clean as it used to do. Oh, that we might change it as we change incompetent washerwomen. Ablution has become pollution.

All these and other changes these two curates saw. We cannot go on. 'Tis not our task—we speak only of that which went on in the neighbourhood of the church. Piccadilly and Lever's

Row and Oldham-street, just become a public thoroughfare ; all is too far away. We must leave them without a notice. Truly in our city churches there is one collect which may well fall with emphasis and meaning on the ears of the devout worshipper—that which speaks of "the changes and chances of this mortal life." *

The last of these chances we must note is the archdeacon's death. He died October 9, 1785. The *Manchester Mercury*, of October 11, speaking of the event, says: "Sunday, died at Neston, in Cheshire, after a long and painful illness, the Rev. Abel Ward, M.A., Archdeacon of Chester, and forty years Rector of St. Ann's in this town. A most exemplary man, both in his public and private life."† He was succeeded in the archdeaconry by Mr. Taylor, rector of Aldford; and in the rectorship by the Rev. Rowland Sandford, junior curate.

Mr. Ward's connection with Chester as prebend in 1744, and archdeacon in 1751, has never died out. It was carried on in his family. In gratitude to the bishop, he baptised one of his elder children, the eldest of those who survived their infancy, by the name of Peploe. He was enrolled at an early age among the scholars of the Manchester School. From Cambridge he entered the Church, took a doctor's degree, and died as prebendary of Ely, and rector of Beeton Cottenham in 1819. A younger brother of Peploe Ward's was Thomas, who, after leaving the Grammar School, went, like his brother, to

---

* We must not suppose that Manchester had yet jumped into a teeming city. An epitaph will correct any such idea. "Here was interred John Willatt, postmaster of the town, who departed this life July 24, 1772, aged 41 years. Also, Sarah Willatt, his wife, late postmistress of this town, who departed this life 25th Dec., 1801, aged 70 years." Imagine a woman single-handed attending to the postal department of Manchester !

† The absence of any reference to his political life shows how completely the old spirit had died out. To the new generation all had become but a tradition.

Cambridge; and, like his father, ended his student career as Fellow of Queen's College. This was in 1777. Indeed, he succeeded his father step by step. He was made prebendary of Chester; and, on the death of the archdeacon, was preferred by the dean and chapter to the vicarage of Neston. He was also a pluralist, being already in possession of the rectorship of Handley. At the time of his death he was vice-dean of the cathedral. Like his father, too, he ended his days at Neston. He was 71 years old, and died in 1827.*

The family vault of the Wards lay beneath St. Mary's Chapel in Chester Cathedral. There the archdeacon himself lies. During the alterations that have been taking place under the careful zeal of the present dean, it was found desirable to re-floor the chapel, and the epitaphs have been removed. , But all memory of those that lie below is not gone. A brass tablet on the wall has an inscription which commemorates the family.† There still lives one direct male representative. Thomas Peploe Ward, Esq., he who set up the tablet afore-mentioned, dwells under the very shadow of that cathedral over which so many of his ancestors have been ministers in more or less high offices for wellnigh a century. His name is a memorial of family associations that are nearly 150 years old. In his surname he can but see a record of much true and laudable service done to the Church of his country. In his second name there must needs

---

* A few days before the archdeacon died, one of his curates, either Mr. Hall or Mr. Sandford, baptised Thomas Quincey, whose parents dwelt in the parish, before they removed to Greenheys. Afterwards as Thomas de Quincey, the opium-eater, he made himself an everlasting name. His father, Thomas Quincey, whose grave is adjacent to those of the two first rectors, is several times mentioned in the *Mercury*, once as declining part of his business, and again as subscribing £10. 10s. to the repeal of the Fustian Tax. He died July 18, 1793, aged 40 years.

† A grand-daughter of the archdeacon married Charles Hamilton, Esq. His son, the Rev. Peploe William Hamilton, died April 1, 1854, being then perpetual curate of Goulden Sutton, near Chester.

be suggested to his mind recollections of that staunch and loyal Whig bishop, Samuel Peploe, who, so early as 1715, began his career at Preston by praying for the reigning family in the very face of the Pretender. Thus do we link name to name. Thus do we carry on from generation to generation these silent, and yet eloquent memorials of high deeds and noble service.

VI.

MANCHESTER SUNDAY SCHOOLS.

RCHDEACON WARD was succeeded at St. Ann's by his junior curate, the Rev. Rowland Sandford. It is not our intention to say anything about Mr. Sandford's ministry at St. Ann's. The great feature of it was the institution and consolidation of the Sunday School system in Manchester. St. Ann's was closely associated with the new movement, Mr. Hall and Mr. Sandford being two of the earliest secretaries to the general committee. A brief account of the rise of these schools in the neighbourhood will not be displeasing to the reader. The Sunday School institution is so firmly grafted upon our English life, so solidly established, that it is hard to think that its birth, its growth, and its strength are of yesterday; and that of it may be almost said that which has been declared of the Temple—

Like some tall palm the noiseless fabric sprung.

Whatever faults may attach to the system, and there are not a few, still we believe the hand of God has been upon it, and made it a blessing.

The casual reader of the *Manchester Mercury* from 1755 to 1784 may be somewhat puzzled by seeing advertisements of special sermons to be preached, and particular hymns to be sung by the charity schools. And it will be as well to explain at once that much that surrounds our great local institution of school anniversaries is only a graft. For at least 140 years Lancashire has had school anniversaries, children specially dressed, tunes specially learnt, and the parish poet beating his brains to compose a special hymn. The charity school was the day school of the period, Sunday differing from week-day in that the children were marshalled to church, where often they were catechised. Benefactions were continually being made for the purpose of educating the children of the poor. William Baguley, the donor of the land whereon St. Ann's was built, left £200 for such an object. In process of time the Collegiate Church, St. Ann's, St. John's, and St. Mary's had each its charity school, depending for existence partly on benefactions, partly on subscriptions, and partly on an annual collection. Every year in due course finds the Rev. Samuel Hall preaching a sermon at St. Ann's for its charity school.*

* The manner in which these schools were supported in Manchester is related by Mr. Bennett, in his sermon at St. Mary's, October 2, 1785. The preacher says: "There is one regulation in Manchester which deserves the attention of every other part of the kingdom, where not already adopted. It is not unusual in many places for the churchwardens and ministers to distribute the offertory money amongst the poor and necessitous people that may casually attend the service. It was once so here. But the benefaction could be but small, the relief transient; clamorous might take place of modest poverty, and artificial sorrow is often louder than real. . . . Hence a resolution passed to devote it to educating poor boys and girls. One of these charity schools is connected to every church; and in this decent and orderly town, where the sacraments are monthly, and where it is not uncommon to see 150 communicants at the altar, the fund is generally found sufficient. The children are occasionally catechised (in church) by the minister." This sermon is entitled: "The advantage of Sunday Schools, a discourse preached for the benefit of that useful and excellent charity, at St. Mary's Church, in Manchester, on Sunday, the 2nd of October, 1785. By the Rev. John Bennett, secretary to the society. Printed by C. Wheeler, and sold by J. Clark and all the booksellers in Manchester." This is probably the *earliest printed sermon* on *Sunday Schools*. It may be seen in the Chetham Library.

In many places, as in our Blue Coat Schools, the boys and girls were provided with a particular dress.* In not a few places they were even housed and fed. Till the close of the last century these seminaries were all but wholly in the hands of the Church of England. The education of the poor was entirely left to her. The denominations were content to leave it so, and the Church was energetic enough to make it so.

The advertisements of these schools and the annual statement read strangely to modern ears. Nor would the amount of learning required, or range of subjects imposed, satisfy our school boards or Church school managers. Both (to think of such a possibility !) would be at one here. The statement of the Lancaster Charity School for 1775, with an original hymn for the service appended, says :—" By this charitable institution forty poor girls are now annually cloathed, furnished with books, taught to read, knit, sew, and spin ; and that they may become useful servants are also instructed in the necessary parts of household work. By a particular recommendation of the subscribers to this charity the trustees this year agreed to furnish each of the girls (beside their usual cloathing) with a substantial blue cloke and hood, and also to purchase six spinning wheels." A sermon for the boys' charity school is also announced in the same year. A special hymn of course occurs, beginning—

'Tis gratitude inspires the song,
   And prompts our annual lay ;
Our grateful strains to heaven belong—
   Our strains to heaven we pay.

* " For the said boys green ffrocks, and with hats, stocks, stockings, and shoes when they have their green ffrocks." " And for the said girls green gowns, and also caps and handkerchiefs, stockings and shoes, when they have their green gowns."—Stretford School, endowed by Mrs. Anne Hinde, by will dated February 11, 1724. Forwarded to me by J. E. Bailey, Esq., F.S.A.

To "pay strains" is strained enough. But the poet no doubt had to strain hard for a rhyme. The behaviour of the boys is said to have improved, and their progress in "reading, writing, and accompts" is equally satisfactory.*

A third "Statement" in 1777 has a hymn on liberality. Indeed, every such hymn at this time was nothing more than an ode to charity, and was wholly Pagan.

As when kind Heaven profusely pours
On thirsty earth refreshing showers,
     The laughing fields rejoice ;
So we for all your kindness raise
The annual hymn of infant praise,
     And swell our grateful voice.

Let mean Ambition's servile train,
Their visionary toys to gain,
     Unceasing vigils keep ;
Let Pleasure's vot'ries ev'ry joy,
Which sober Reason owns, destroy,
     To eat, to drink, to sleep.

Let misers, grasping still at more,
To add to their superfluous store,
     Each liberal thought repress ;
While you with open hand shall give,
And all the heart-felt joys receive
     Which gen'rous bosoms bless.

While Heaven, propitious on your toil,
Shall, as the gen'rous widows' oil,
     Your property increase ;
And, as life's bustling scene decays,
Benignant bless its closing days
     With Plenty, Health, and Peace.

And so on in a highly moral strain—not a word that a conscientious Hottentot could not have consented to sing; the

---

* The above is extracted from the papers of the Rev. Thomas Wilson, Master of the Clitheroe Grammar School, 1775. Canon Raines printed a selection for the Chetham Society in 1857.

I

sermon, we doubt not, of the same sort. Truly, such evangelists as Whitfield and Grimshaw did not arise up too soon. The above, however, is a fair sample of the rhyming power of the day. A very pretentious hymn, sung in 1783, a year before the Sunday School anniversaries began, and occupied their place, concludes—

> To Him who reigns enthroned above,
> Hope's tri-une God, the Source of love,
>   The glorious Trinity :
> While earth doth last, when planets fall,
> When pristine chaos buries all,
>   Eternal praises be !

Nevertheless, these charity schools were few and far between, and although in many cases attendance upon public worship on Sunday was compulsory, the vast body of young people in our large centres was untouched. The deadness of religion, both in our churches and chapels in the first half of the eighteenth century, had begun to tell fearfully upon the youth of the country. There was no hand to guide their feet to the sanctuary. They collected about the street corners, scoffed at the church-goer, grovelled in the actual and moral mud of the courts and alleys in which they lived, and were only conscious of the Sabbath institution as a day upon which they could untrammel themselves from all fetters. Robert Raikes has the credit of first introducing the Sunday School into England, the month of November, 1780, as he himself declares, being the time of the commencement of his work in Gloucester. He got four women to take in as many boys and girls as he could collect—paying each a shilling a Sunday for their work. They were to teach reading and the catechism. A visible improvement in the Sunday aspect of the town was immediately apparent. The success of the experiment becoming known, Leeds took the initiative in the north, and Manchester followed. The history of the Manchester Sunday Schools so naturally divides itself into three epochs that for the sake of perspicuity we may as well separate them. Each marks a crisis. If we must give them names we can term them severally the Town Committee, the Church Committee, and Local Committees.

(a) THE TOWN COMMITTEE.

On the 10th August, 1784, the boroughreeve and constables, Thomas Johnson, John Kearsley, and Henry Norris, issued an address to the public, recommending the establishment of Sunday Schools. This is said—though there is no proof for the statement—to have been done at the instance of Dr. Bayley, rector of St. James's. It is worth while quoting it at full :—

"Aug. 10th, 1784, Manchester.

"The boroughreeve and constables of Manchester beg leave to recommend the following address to the notice of the public. The plan of establishing Sunday Schools meets with their hearty approbation, and they should be happy, in concurrence with the principal inhabitants of the town, to lend their assistance and support to so laudable a charity.

"THOMAS JOHNSON, Boroughreeve.
"JOHN KEARSLEY, }
"HENRY NORRIS, } Constables."

Then follows "An Address to the Public on Sunday Schools." After a word or two on the importance of education, it thus proceeds :—"The neglect of it (education) is one principal cause of the misery of families, cities, and nations : ignorance, vice, and misery being constant companions. The hardest heart must melt at the melancholy sight of such a multitude of children, both male and female, in this town, who live in gross ignorance, infidelity, and habitual profanation of the Lord's Day. What crowds fill the streets ! tempting each other to idleness, play, lewdness, and every other species of wickedness . . . To attempt a remedy is laudable and divine.

"Some time ago the clergy-man of Stroud, in Gloucestershire, began an institution which was called a Sunday School, and which has been attended with happy consequences. Since then a clergy-man of Leeds adopted the same institution, and others have followed his example, and improved his plan.

"The present state of the Sunday School at Leeds is to this purpose: The town being divided into seven divisions has in it twenty-six schools, forty-four or forty-five masters, above 2,000 scholars, each master having about forty under his care." A number of particulars follow. The Leeds custom is for children to come at one and stay under supervision "till evening comes on." They are first conducted to the afternoon church. They are brought back, and taught "reading, writing, and the principles of Christianity." A form of prayer is used to conclude the school meeting. There are "Inquisitors" appointed to visit the different schools every Sunday. The schools are hired (that is, rooms are rented in dwelling-houses) at £1. 10s. per annum, or £1. 1s. or 15s. The expenses of their first year are stated to be £23, to be met by subscriptions. The address concludes by declaring that already in Manchester this plan has been adopted by several people, and that a book for subscriptions to meet present and future expenses has been left open at the Exchange Coffee House.

Six weeks after the promulgation of this address (28th September, 1784), a large meeting was held at the Bull's Head, in the Market Place. Sir John Parker Mosley, a regular attendant at St. Ann's, was made president; G. Lloyd and T. Johnson, vice-presidents; Rev. J. Bennett, secretary; and Mr. James Dinwiddie, treasurer. As deputy treasurers, Richard Barlow represented Christ Church; Richard Kearsley, St. Ann's; John Ridings, St. Mary's; Richard Keymer, St. John's; and William Wright, St. Paul's. The general committee included John Kearsley, and Henry Norris (chief constables), Sir Ashton Lever (Lever-street), Samuel Clowes

(Broughton), Rev. John Clowes (St. John's), the Rev. John Bennett, Henry Barton (Swinton), John Entwistle (Bank, King-street), Robert Markland, and T. Phillips. Thus the principal inhabitants undoubtedly came forward. It was stated that some thousands of books had been already purchased. Subscriptions are earnestly solicited.

Certainly help must have been needed. A week before this, September 21, it was stated in the public papers that "the rapid progress of Sunday Schools in this town promises the most salutary results. There are now begun no less than 25 of them in different parts, attended by nearly 1,800 children! The change already worked in the manners of these untaught wanderers is truly delightful. Instead of their usual slovenly appearance, they now vie with each other in coming to school as neat and clean as their situations will allow."*

It is clear that Manchester began well. The honour of initiating the movement belongs to Col. Richard Townley. So early as Jan. 6, 1784, a letter appears in the *Manchester Mercury*, addressed to that gentleman by Robert Raikes himself. It is dated from Gloucester, Nov. 25, 1783. He thus describes his work then :—"The beginning of this scheme was entirely owing to accident. Some business leading me one morning into the suburbs of the city, where the lowest of the people (principally employed in the pin manufactory) chiefly reside, I was struck with concern at seeing a groupe of children wretchedly ragged at play in the street. . . . 'Ah, sir,' said the woman to whom I was speaking, 'could you take a view of this part of the town on a Sunday, you would be shocked

---

* The Manchester mode of operation seems to have met with approval throughout the country. Not more than twelve months after the committee had been established Mr. Bennett speaks of "the number of applications which have been received by our society at Manchester for a specimen of our plan from many parts of the kingdom, and from some quarters of Wales."—*Vide* sermon at St. Mary's already quoted.

indeed, for then the street is filled with multitudes of these wretches, who, released on that day from employment, spend their time in noise and riot, playing at chuck, and cursing and swearing in a manner so horrid as to convey to my serious mind an idea of hell rather than any other place.' . . . I then enquired of the woman if there were any decent, well-disposed women in the neighbourhood who kept schools for teaching to read.   I presently was directed to four.   To these I applied, and made an agreement with them to receive as many children as I should send upon the Sunday, whom they were to instruct in reading and in the Church Catechism.   For this I engaged to pay them each a shilling for their day's employment."   The women were pleased, the clergyman of the parish lent his assistance, and order and decorum, Mr. Raikes adds, were obtained even "among such a set of little heathens" as these. "It is now about three years since we began."*   The place "has become quite a heaven upon Sundays," says an old woman quoted by Mr. Raikes.   "On Sunday afternoon they are marched to church ; but, what is more extraordinary, these little ragamuffins have in great number taken it into their heads to frequent the early morning prayers at seven o'clock in the Cathedral.   I believe there were nearly fifty this morning. . . . The great principle I inculcate is to be kind and good-natured to each other, not to provoke one another; to be dutiful to their parents, not to offend God by cursing and swearing. The number at present attending are about 250 ; the number increasing every week."   It is a great pleasure to him, he adds, to study the little ones.   "It is botanizing in human nature." The one rule of entrance is "clean hands, clean face, and hair combed."   Robert Raikes concludes by hoping that such a scheme may be begun in Manchester, and meet with like success.

* Thus we get the exact date, Nov. 1780.   This settles a much debated question.

The result of the publication of this letter was the address put forth by the boroughreeve and constables nine months later. Col. Townley was ardently supported by Mr. Bennett, the rector of St. Mary's. To these two gentlemen is unmistakeably due the merit of commencing a scheme of Sunday school instruction in Manchester.

The next meeting of the general committee was held Nov. 1. Sir John Mosley in the chair. It was resolved that "a separate committee be appointed for each of the five districts into which the town is divided," to test the abilities of the masters and mistresses. It was further resolved to open no fresh schools from that date without the approbation of the committee. Lastly, it was resolved that a form of rules for the government of all these schools be printed. It will interest many, if we give the names of the several sub-committees.

Christ Church District. — Messrs. Houghton, Henry Barton, Dauntsey Holme, George Bramall, William Wright, Loxham, Briarley, and George Walker.

St. Mary's District.—Messrs. Robert Markland, John Ridings, Thomas Philips, James Ackers, Jonathan Beever, Fullerton, and Rev. J. Bennett.

St. John's District.—Rev. Mr. Clowes, Messrs. G. Lloyd, Charles Wood, Richard Keymer, Kinder, and Peter Wright.

St. Ann's District.—Rev. Mr. Hall, Rev. Dr. Barnes,* Messrs. John Entwistle, James Dinwiddie, James Potter, Samuel Mather, and Richard Powell.

St. Paul's District.—Messrs. Johnson, James Barton, Poole, Hudson, Brocklehurst, Wittenbury, James Clough,† and James Hurst.

As a proof of the good effected, we may quote a letter of " Benevolus," (Mr. Bennett ?) April 12, 1785, four months after

* Minister of the Cross-street Chapel.

† Much of the extraordinary success attending St. Paul's schools was the work of James Clough.

the institution had been at work. "To remove these difficulties (the want and necessities of the poor) the plan of Sunday Schools was suggested, and immediately adopted in almost every quarter of the kingdom. It was one of those happy thoughts which common sense approves. In Manchester, in particular, it was embraced, and patronised with that ardour which becomes a good cause. A liberal contribution was made, and no less than thirty schools opened under the care of proper teachers." He concludes by bewailing the carelessness of parents who do not seize advantage of the boon, and by earnestly beseeching them not to lose such an opportunity.

To tell the story of the Manchester Sunday School movement is to record the march of an army victorious at every turn.*   It was begun on the broadest of bases.   Churchmen,

* It may interest the reader to learn the exact date of the rise of some of the Sunday Schools of the neighbourhood. I have gleaned my information from the local papers of the time. Chapel-en-le-Frith began its school in January, 1785, under the patronage of Samuel Frith, the late High Sheriff. There must have been a school at Hollinwood in August, 1784, for it is reported on the 17th of that month that "Mr. Raikes of Gloucester has presented 100 spelling books to the Minister for the use of the children in the Sunday Schools there." Walkden Moor school opened 22nd August, 1784. The first Sunday 100 attended; second, 120; third, 140. A school at Bury is announced in the papers of August 31. The Methodists of Rochdale began about August 24th; 276 children came. Beeston began on Trinity Sunday, in the same year, with 217 scholars. On April 11th, 1786, a Sunday School is reported open at Gateshead Mill, Saddleworth. It was established by Mr. Buckley for the mill hands. Mossley schools, begun about the close of the same month, had 400 children in attendance by the middle of June. Denton and Haughton opened in May. Ardwick Chapel (St. Thomas') in June. In Monton, Worsley, and Swinton, schools were established in October, 1785. In the two latter about 250 children were in attendance. Middleton, Chadderton, and Tonge, began in the spring of 1786. By midsummer 200 scholars were on the rolls. Altrincham and Bowdon began in May, 1785, with 120 children. In August, 1786, there were 1,200 children in the five schools at Bolton. Prestwich, under Mr. Lyon, began in January of the same year. Heaton Norris began

Dissenters, and Roman Catholics sat on the committee. Every child was at liberty to attend such place of worship in the afternoon as its parents desired—only the condition was it must go to some service. The catechism was taught only to children of the Established Church. In December, 1784, the Collegiate Church district had seven different rooms in use, one in Fennel-street, Rooden Gutter, Miller's Lane, Clock Alley, Red Bank, and two in Cold-house. St. Mary's had three, all in Parsonage. St. John's had four, one in Cumberland-street and Jackson's Row, and two in Tickle-street. St. Ann's had two, one in Brown-street, a second in Tickle-street, at the upper end. St. Paul's had ten, one at the back of the Saracen's Head, Paradise, Tib-street, Turner-street, Thomas-street, Spittal Fields, Oldham-street, and three in Newton Lane (Oldham Road). Mrs. Trimmer's "Guide to Servants," Dr. Watts' "Divine Songs," and Foxe's "Historical Lessons" were used, and soon 3,000 children were in attendance. In 1789 there were more than forty rooms in private dwelling-houses in use.

Of course, the masters and mistresses, with their under-teachers, were paid for their services. No master was to have more than forty children under his care. At first the salary was 2s. a Sunday for head-teachers, 1s. 6d. for under-teachers. This was reduced by-and-by to 1s. 6d. and 1s. Every district had its special visitors or inquisitors, whose duty it was to visit

September, 1785 ; 134 children. The first anniversary of Parish Church schools, Ashton, was in September, 1786 ; 500 children. Rev. Samuel Hall, curate of St. Ann's, delivered the discourse. Birch and Oldham had their first anniversary in the first week of October, 1786. Mr. Assheton, of the Collegiate Church, pleaded the cause at the latter. Mr. Bennett preached the first anniversary sermon at Hindley, near Wigan, in October, 1786. The advertisement says:—"A select number of boys and girls from St. Mary's, Manchester, will attend to sing such psalms and hymns as are suitable to the occasion ; and some striking parts of the Messiah and other oratorios will be interspersed through the service by several of the best vocal performers of Hindley." Reading and writing was taught at all.

the several schools, Sunday by Sunday, to inform the committee of abuses, to suggest improvements, and to criticise the work of both teachers and scholars. The visitors for St. Ann's district were James and Thomas Potter, Dr. Barnes, of the Cross Street Chapel, and the Rev. Samuel Hall, of St. Ann's. Until the disruption in 1800, a collection was made in every church and chapel in rotation, beginning with the Collegiate Church the first Sunday in September, and ending with the Methodist chapel in Oldham Street at the end of October. Every sermon was to be preached at the afternoon service, and all hymns sung were to be under the supervision of the head committee. Hymn books for schools were not priced at one penny then. The cheapest was a shilling per copy.

To the honour of Manchester, be it said, that so early as September 6th, 1786, a rule was passed that no writing was henceforward to be taught in the school-room, and it was specially stated by the committee that reading was only retained that the children might be led to understand the better, and peruse for themselves at home the religious books lent or given to them, and also that they might more heartily and sensibly join in the services of the sanctuary. The rule about writing, however, only extended to the schools of this committee.*

Mr. Hall was general secretary of the institution four or five times, the appointment being an annual one. Mr. Sandford also took the post twice. The year he died, 1795, we find that he asked to decline the office through ill-health, but being over-persuaded, he accepted the post. He only attended one meeting. He had to leave Manchester to drink the waters at Harrogate, and very soon his place in parish and committee

---

* After the disruption in 1800, writing seems to have crept into both Church and Dissenting schools for a time. Perhaps a feeling of rivalry led to this.

knew him no more.* His widow continued actively to visit the school-room attached to St. John's, and so late as 1816, she, then about seventy-seven years old, with Miss Byrom attended to her duties as lady visitor. In 1789, we find Mr. John Satterfield made visitor to the schools in Blackfriars. For ninety years at least the name has been closely associated with St. Ann's, and from the day that unpaid took the place of salaried teachers, the ranks of St. Ann's little army of Sunday school helpers has constantly been recruited from the establishment that bore that name until two or three years ago.

But we must hurry on. A list of the collections in 1789, 1791, and 1793 may interest the reader. The two chapels in Mosley-street and that in Cannon-street are not mentioned, they having been somewhat remiss at this time.

	1789.			1791.			1793.		
	£	s.	d.	£	s.	d.	£	s.	d.
(1) Old Church	33	3	5	31	7	0	25	16	2
(2) St. Ann's	33	16	9	24	9	8	22	6	7
(3) St. Mary's	33	4	8	49	1	8	23	0	2
(4) St. John's	60	10	6	50	7	10	49	9	5
(5) St. Paul's	89	3	6	74	13	1	61	13	4
(6) Trinity (Salford)	45	6	2	32	7	6	25	3	9
(7) St. James'	73	2	6	62	5	8	66	3	4
(8) St. Michael's	31	18	7	35	10	10	22	6	10
(9) Romish Chapel	36	15	0	30	0	0	22	0	7
(10) Oldham-street Chapel	66	2	0	75	3	3	66	11	10
(11) Salford Methodists	—			30	12	1	20	4	8
	£503	3	1	£495	17	9	£404	16	8

* Mr. Sandford died at Harrogate, June 24th, 1795, after ten years of office. He was buried at St. Ann's, close beside the two first rectors. His epitaph runs thus :—" Here lie the remains of the Rev. Rowland Sandford, A.B., curate and rector of this church during the space of twenty-one years. The various duties of his station, whether those of the master or the man, he discharged with exemplary fidelity and unwearied attention. He died June 24th, 1795, aged 54. Also the body of Mary his wife, who died October 30th, 1817, aged 78 years."

The erection of *special* buildings for Sunday School use was seriously entertained in 1795, a Mr. William Barrow having left a legacy of £100 for such a purpose. Land in Long Millgate was surveyed; but the price wanted for it by Mr. Fawcett, a clergyman in Oldham, was too high; and Mr. Barrow's property having been put into Chancery, which then, if not now, meant that it would be a long time before it got out again, the idea was for the time given up.

The year 1799 was a trying one. Many dissensions arose. Funds decreased, yet the work required an increase. The teachers' salaries were reduced, and they sent a deputation asking for the accustomed stipend. Several rooms had to be given up. Dr. Bayley, of St. James', and Mr. Myddelton, of St. Mary's, whose church collections were among the largest, refused to continue them. They found fault with Mr. Clowes, Mr. Dallas (his curate), and Mr. Randall, the curate in charge of St. Ann's (the rector, Mr. Barker, was a pluralist like Archdeacon Ward), for a real or fancied infringement of the original rules, by which the Church party suffered, and the Dissenters gained an advantage.* A large number of subscriptions fell off. A majority of the general committee absented themselves from the Bull's Head at the monthly meetings. The case was urgent. A special committee was formed to treat with the recalcitrants. The laymen came back; Dr. Bayley † and Mr.

---

* A motion had been carried previously, which practically excluded the children from church. Each child might go to a place of worship once a month, not oftener. If four rooms were in use in a district, one room a Sunday attended the sanctuary. Thus the children were represented at every service but by one-fourth of the entire number only.

† It is a common error to ascribe the honour of introducing Sunday Schools into Manchester to Dr. Bayley, of St. James'. This mistake arose from the fact that his determined opposition in 1799 and 1800 to the then system of government caused the Church and the Nonconforming bodies to separate, and carry on their work independently. Dr. Bayley, in a sense, was the founder of Church Schools in 1800; but to Colonel Townley, of Belfield, and the Rev. John Bennett, of St. Mary's, must be fairly given the greater honour of originating the movement in 1783.

Myddelton were still obdurate. On the 5th May, 1800, that happened which sooner or later must have come about. At a large gathering of the general committee four propositions were carried.

I. That a certain number of the forty or more rooms in use, according to the proportion of money sub-scribed by the Church members, shall be set apart and assigned to the sole government of the clergy and their friends, to be called henceforth Church of England Schools.

II. These schools, as well as the remainder to be attached to the Nonconformist bodies, are to be supported from the general funds.*

III. The clergy are to have sole authority over their own schools; the same right to belong to the Dissenters.

IV. That a select committee be at once formed to make a fair division.

Thus ended the original institution, which had lasted sixteen years, and certainly done its work with energy, if not always with discretion. When the disruption came the Sunday School system had become an established fact. Internal discord could but affect the method; it was powerless to stay, or even hinder the movement. I doubt not the decision come to was a wise one. Certainly, the Church party (I have no figures relating to the other bodies) began at once with larger resources than they had ever hitherto possessed.

(b) THE CHURCH COMMITTEE.

Thomas B. Bayley, Esq., of Hope—the father of Sir Daniel and Archdeacon Bayley—took the chair at the first meeting of what we may call the new organisation. The Warden of the Collegiate Church was made president; the vice-presidents

* This rule evidently fell into abeyance soon afterwards, for a separate subscription list for the Church schools is found so early as 1805.

included George Walker, John Kearsley, Henry Barton, and Edward Place; the committee included the boroughreeve and constables, and the clergy and all subscribers of a guinea and more. The ten parishes were turned into ten districts; the clergy were to be governors of those schools whose children attended their churches. Two visitors or inquisitors were appointed over each district. The names of the four gentlemen who undertook to collect money for the St. Ann's district were Edward Place,* a vice-president, Joseph Armstrong,† John Satterfield, and John Ollivant. The surnames of the latter three are familiar to this day.

The schools of the Establishment obtained distinction by a very politic movement commenced immediately after the separation. It still flourishes as one of the most popular of local institutions. In 1801 took place the first Whit-Monday procession. On the 28th January, at a full meeting, it was decided that the children of all Church Schools in Manchester and Salford should meet in St. Ann's Square, and hear a sermon, and join in Divine Service. On the 24th February, it was further decided that the service should be held in St. Ann's Church, as being most convenient. At the personal request of Warden Blackburne, however, it was gladly changed to the Collegiate Church, and he was asked to preach the first sermon, on Monday, the 6th of May. The best girl singers in each school learnt several special hymns and tunes, and sat by

* So early as 1767, we find Edward Place connected with St. Ann's. "Elizabeth, daughter of Edward and Elizabeth Place, Oct. 11, 1767." (Register of Baptisms, St. Ann's.)

† Son of Joseph Armstrong. (v. page 90.) His father died Jan. 21, 1786. "Died, very much beloved, and regretted by his acquaintance, Mr. Joseph Armstrong, wine and liquor merchant." (*Mercury.*) A daughter is mentioned a year before : "Wednesday, was married at the Collegiate Church, Mr. John Winterbottom, fustian manufacturer, to Miss Armstrong, daughter of Mr. Armstrong, wine and liquor merchant." (*Mercury,* Jan. 11, 1785.)

themselves in the Blue Coat Gallery, and they all received a good scolding from the organist, Mr. Cheese, for their incapacity, Mr. Cheese, like many a great musical genius before him—shall we say after him ?—being of a peculiarly irritable temperament. The procession marched six abreast. The boroughreeve and chief constables went before, " the minstrels followed after," in the shape of the regimental band. The schools came in the rear in this order :—Collegiate Church, St. Ann's, St. Mary's, St. John's, St. Peter's, St. James's, St. Paul's, St. Michael's, the Sacred Trinity, Salford, and St. Stephen's, Salford. About 2,500 children took part. Every teacher was provided after service with cheese and bread. The following year this was changed to "a dinner and a quart of ale each." But the latter rule was quickly rescinded,* for a teacher was brought up for being found drunk and disorderly in the old church-yard. It was ruled that 1s. should be given to every teacher, and an additional 6d. to the master or mistress. Great *eclat* followed this new institution, and to heighten the effect, and to obtain better order and decorum, the committee ordained that the churchwarden and beadles of every church should walk with the scholars, bearing white wands with them, the wands to be provided from the general funds.

It was about the year 1812 or 1813 that Whit-week excursions came into existence. It was found, year by year, that many of the boys, and not a few girls, attended the races on Kersall Moor, and that many evil influences were the result. At first the practice seems to have been to take them on Whit-Wednesday, the chief race day, into the opposite suburb, allowing them to bring or buy their own meal. In 1814, however, the great institution of "buns," if not milk, came into opera-

* In April, 1814, a rule was passed forbidding "liquors on any pretence being taken into the Sunday Schools." I fear the paid teachers had had an occasional quart brought in. That was not difficult, while the rooms lay over the stables of several of the inns and hostelries of the town.

tion,* the excursions were lengthened, Dunham Park and Flixton, and later on Southport, were visited by the canal boats, for want of railway trains, and Whit-week, as understood by modern Lancashire people, was gradually brought into existence. I believe the larger schools attached to St. Paul's, were the first to originate this movement. That few will be found who will not confess that Whit-week is overdone, and that certain evils have become associated with its festivities only less by comparison than those very evils they were intended to counteract, I firmly believe.† Nevertheless I do not see any reason why these evils should not be removed, and Whit-week made a time of really innocent recreation to the thousands who have to pass the year in the dark courts and gloomy alleys of our crowded centres.

I have in my possession, a document‡—perhaps unique—a report of the state of our Manchester Church Schools from 1805 to 1810. It is in the form of a large double sheet, and contains an address to the public, a list of officers, visitors, and superintendents, a statement of accounts, and the names of

---

* The first mention of edibles for the children is in 1814. The committee ordered "a number of cakes to be baked at 1d. each for the children," to be eaten on Whit-Monday before starting for St. Ann's Square. In 1821 this had become a sufficiently recognised custom for a further rule, demanding that they should be made "at 9d. per dozen." In that year they are called "buns." In 1823 the committee issued an order for "4,800 buns to be baked." Buns were popular.

† One most glaring evil is the long distance to which children are often taken. They start at dawn, and return at midnight. Neither physical nor moral good can result.

‡ I am indebted to Mr. Edmund Mason (of Messrs. Holgate, St. Mary's Gate), for this interesting document. It was discovered in the wall behind a cupboard during some alterations. The Messrs. Holgate, of 1805-10, are found among the subscribers. Hence their possession of a copy. Mr. John Holgate took sole management of the anniversary music at Collegiate Church in 1819, by special request of the committee.

over 1000 subscribers to the general fund, the sums collected
in the different churches, including the Whit-Monday offertory,
and, what is still more valuable, an authentic list of the existing
schools, the streets in which they are situated, and the number
of the house.* The address is carefully written. It declares that
no scheme has been found so conducive to the instruction of
the poor in the knowledge of their God and Saviour as Sunday
Schools. "If they (the children) are induced to love God, to
honour His holy name, and to follow the precepts of that religion which animates us to a holy course of living, and thus
prepares us for the enjoyment of eternal happiness in the future
life, we must ever admire the wisdom and the design of Sunday
Schools! . . . An experience of nearly thirty years† has sufficiently shown to its most zealous friends and supporters its
intrinsic value, notwithstanding all the objections which have
been urged against them."‡

I subjoin a list of churches and collections from 1805 to
1810.

* This part of the report will be found in Appendix 2.

† Twenty-seven years.   The committee could certainly look back
with undisguised satisfaction upon the work accomplished.   The success of
the Manchester Sunday School movement, at such an early stage of its
history, must be attributed very largely to the fact that it was made a
Town question, as well as a Church question.   It had not merely been
patronised by the leading official dignitaries of the place, but they had
themselves entered heartily into its practical conduct.   So early as May 30,
1786, the local print quotes the London papers as declaring that Manchester
is taking the "lead of all the kingdom in the business of Sunday Schools,"
adding that there are 1,542 boys, 1,294 girls, and that £1,000 have been
collected for their support.

‡ We may here state that all the Town Committee meetings had been
held at the "Bull's Head."   In 1800 the new Church Committee met at
the "Star Inn," in Deansgate.   A year or two later we find them at the
"Coach and Horses Inn," in the same street.   Eventually a room in the
Police Court was allotted them.

J

Years ending 30th June.		1805. £	s.	d.	Scholars.	1806. £	s.	d.	Scholars.	1807. £	s.	d.	Scholars.
Collegiate Church	Sermon..	21	17	1	260	27	6	0	260	23	8	0	192
	Subscrip	79	9	6		68	0	0		120	10	0	
St. Ann's ..	Sermon..	28	1	9	321	22	3	5	130	28	1	1	103
	Subscrip.	65	6	6		75	15	6		74	13	0	
St. Mary's ..	Sermon..	28	4	10	270	29	7	0	270	27	19	4	270
	Subscrip	54	11	0		47	13	6		53	6	6	
St. Paul's ...	Sermon..	31	10	10	1763	35	2	10	1890	33	11	1	2029
	Subscrip	57	11	2		72	14	0		94	0	0	
St. John's ...	Sermon..	62	9	0	475	52	14	9	480	52	1	3	428
	Subscrip.	30	0	0		33	13	6		37	17	0	
St. James's..	Sermon..	93	2	3	300	78	9	8	290	76	5	11	350
	Subscrip.	30	14	0		27	17	0		25	4	6	
St Michael's	Sermon..	21	11	7	385	15	3	7	398	23	12	5	450
	Subscrip.	16	0	0		18	0	3		15	8	6	
St. Peter's...	Sermon..	32	6	10	293	27	7	1	570	22	12	2	639
	Subscrip	19	18	0		20	8	6		19	8	6	
Trinity	Sermon..	23	17	1	311	26	2	5	324	17	12	6	327
	Subscrip.	35	16	6		32	5	6		39	17	0	
St. Stephen's	Sermon..	18	15	10	746	37	7	6	748	33	6	11	836
	Subscrip	57	7	6		63	13	0		76	6	0	
Legacies		20	0	0	...	...	...		...	146	9	0	...
Anniversary Sermon ...		66	16	6	..	56	3	0	...	55	3	5	...
Total of Scholars each Year......................		...	...		5124	...	...		5360	...	...		5624
Total Receipts...		895	7	9	...	847	8	0	...	1096	5	1	...
Total Payments		853	0	0	...	812	6	7	...	1044	5	4	...
Fund increased		42	7	9	...	55	1	5	...	51	19	9	...
Fund reduced		...	...		...	...	...		...	...	...		...

Years ending 30th June.		1808. £	s.	d.	Scholars.	1809. £	s.	d.	Scholars.	1810. £	s.	d.	Scholars.
Collegiate Church	Sermon..	33	7	5	268	32	5	6	230	39	19	0	259
	Subscrip.	99	12	6		93	7	0		78	14	6	
St. Ann's ...	Sermon..	30	4	10	129	37	9	0	115	37	0	5	127
	Subscrip.	64	7	0		61	12	6		60	10	0	
St. Mary's...	Sermon..	40	12	3	270	35	3	7	250	34	15	5	260
	Subscrip.	55	14	0		100	16	2		92	3	6	
St. Paul's ...	Sermon..	27	2	10	2455	26	16	4	2441	29	9	3	2921
	Subscrip.	96	14	3		83	13	0		125	7	3	
St. John's ...	Sermon..	50	4	9	396	47	16	3	520	50	11	10	540
	Subscrip.	38	7	0		54	3	0		50	4	9	
St. James's..	Sermon..	82	11	8	405	73	13	1	420	92	0	0	420
	Subscrip.	30	5	0		35	11	0		31	4	9	
St. Michael's	Sermon..	14	1	9	538	14	14	5	588	16	6	7	770
	Subscrip.	14	2	6		17	6	10		18	10	6	
St. Peter's...	Sermon..	22	0	6	893	30	5	0	774	33	6	6	755
	Subscrip.	53	4	0		39	19	6		24	17	0	
Trinity	Sermon..	25	6	5	388	15	0	0	430	15	18	11	433
	Subscrip.	40	11	0		41	3	6		34	7	6	
St. Stephen's	Sermon..	40	10	0	915	34	0	5	912	34	1	7	939
	Subscrip.	82	8	0		96	8	6		94	8	0	
Legacies		18	0	0	...	45	0	0	...	...	...	...	...
Anniversary Sermon ...		52	2	1	...	62	17	0	...	61	16	8	...
Total of Scholars each Year		...	...	...	6657	...	...	...	6680	...	...	...	7424
Total Receipts		1011	9	9	...	1079	1	7	...	1055	13	11	...
Total Payments		990	0	1	...	1071	10	5	...	1284	5	4	...
Fund increased		21	9	8	...	7	11	2	...	...	...	...	...
Fund reduced		...	...	...	...	...	...	...	...	228	11	5	...

Although the debit and credit account is not quite so satisfactory as might have been wished, this report must have been of a most encouraging character. In 1793 the total receipts from churches and chapels together came to but £404. Nearly treble that sum is now credited to the Church account alone. In 1801 about 2,500 children walked in the procession. In 1810 the number of scholars had swelled to 7,424.

It is curious to note the items of expenditure. The teachers' salaries, together with rents, coals, and candles, amount to £786. 2s. 3d., a serious item in those days. It has well been said that there were only two good grounds for supposing at one time that the Sunday School movement would decline. The moral effect of such a system could never be what it ought to be so long as teaching was looked upon as a professed occupation. Yet Mr. Raikes himself never contemplated any other method than that of paid teaching. In "Chambers' Encyclopædia" I see the year 1800 set down as the period when this evil was generally removed. This is a great mistake. Till 1812, at least, the custom was all but universal. The writer of the article is obliged to admit that, after Raikes' death in 1811, the schools at Gloucester were obliged to be closed for want of funds, the expenses of teaching being so great. The employment of gratuitous labour, however, began, and a most beneficial consequence was the effect. Our Sunday Schools started on a new career of success; a higher class of teachers proffered their services; a higher class of scholars attended the schools. The public was more satisfied as to the reality of the movement; the building of schools to be devoted solely to the work was inaugurated; it was, in fact, a new system, and a fresh impetus was given to the institution.*

* An alteration in the places of meeting had taken place. The Collegiate Church School was in Fennel-street. St. Ann's had two rooms in Tib Lane; St. Mary's, two rooms in the Star Inn Yard; St. Paul's, one in Gun-street, Turner-street, Silk-street, Jersey-street, and George Leigh-

Many, many years, however, passed away before gratuitous instruction became universal; and I believe several schools could at this moment be found (though not in the Manchester diocese) where paid labour has not become obsolete. It was long, too, before writing was abolished; reading still prevails, in spite of our many night schools. Perhaps School Boards will stop this. I remember my father's old friend, the Rev. George Docker Grundy, perhaps the most successful parish clergyman in the north of England, saying that, when he came to Hey, near Oldham, in 1837, he met with much abuse for abolishing writing lessons on the Lord's day. When he visited the cottages the children shouted after him—

> Here comes the Reverend Mister Grundy,
> Who'll ha' no writing upon a Sunday.

He quickly laid down this hindrance to his popularity, however; and at the age of 70, without a curate, carries on his Sunday services in three different buildings. On Easter Sunday he had over 300 communicants after morning service.

Whit-Monday, 1815, a few days before the battle of Waterloo, was very memorable for a sad accident attending the anniversary. The Collegiate Church had long needed repairs, the galleries being especially rickety. A scheme was then afoot to renew the interior, which was carried out at a cost of £20,000. Just before the sermon a cry was raised that the roof was coming in. A scene followed baffling description. The children fled the church, a crush ensued, and a little boy was killed, five being borne to the Infirmary in an injured state. A special meeting

street. These two latter must have been in factories, for one had 684 children; the other, 1,526. St. John's had a room holding 540; St. James' had two separate rooms in Portland-street; St. Michael's, two in Miller-street; St. Peter's, one in Jackson's Row, and another in Alport Town; Trinity, one in the Workhouse, a second in the King's Head Yard; and St. Stephen's, one in Bloom-street, another in Oldfield Lane—in all twenty-one different tenements.

was called in the afternoon, and after formally thanking Mr.
Mallory, one of the fellows, for the sermon he had not been
able to preach, it was agreed that as all kinds of exaggerated
rumours were afloat, placards should be issued the same evening
to allay the general consternation by a strict narration of the
truth.   The five children quickly recovered, and Waterloo cast
all other topics, and this with it, into oblivion.   Not so with
the Committee.   It was ruled that the Whit-Monday anniversary should cease.   In future it was to be held on the Sunday
after Ascension Day; only St. Ann's and St. Mary's schools
were to meet in the Square, the rest at Piccadilly, St. Peter's
meadow, and the Collegiate churchyard, according to their   .
contiguity to the same.   Four sermons were to be preached
at the four nearest churches to these four points.   St. Ann's
and St. James's broke this rule the first year by omitting any
gathering at all.   The plan, when carried out, failed to attract
the public attention and to touch the public pockets, and in
1819 the Committee were glad to rescind their resolution and
allow the old state of things to be renewed.

In 1813, the first rule was laid down respecting the dress
of the children.   Fault had been found with the flounces and
bonnets worn by many of the girls.   In the April of this year
it was ordered that the girls should be clad in "caps and
tippets of a plain and modest character."*   There must be "an
uniform attire," and "all finery and gaudy decorations will be
a bar to walking in the procession."   For a meeting of grave
and sober and reverend divines, the resolution is not badly
expressed.   At least it is better than the one passed six years
later, that "no immoderate or indecorous extravagance of dress
in the females be allowed."   The reverend committee must

* We must not suppose that "caps and tippets" were a new institution. They have been worn in Manchester for at least one hundred years, at
the charity sermons and afterwards at the Sunday School anniversaries of
the separate churches.

have come fresh from a perusal of the Latin Fathers, I should say. Only the *Daily Telegraph* could afford to be so ponderous in the present day. In this same year, 1819, the schools for the first time took the route still followed in 1876, King-street, York-street, Mosley-street, Market-street.* In the Market Place, the elder children marched to the right to the Collegiate Church, the little ones to the left into St. Ann's Square, and thence to their homes again. Previously the march had been direct from the Square to the Old Church. While on the subject of dress, we may add that great consternation was caused in this same year, 1819, from the fact that many of the boys were sent by their fathers and mothers in drab coloured hats, and other badges of the disaffected and riotous townspeople. Great indignation was expressed by the more loyal inhabitants, the matter was taken up, and the practice straitly forbidden.

(*c*) LOCAL COMMITTEES.

In 1839 the union terminated. We need not enter too particularly into the cause that led to the disruption. Sufficient to say that out of twenty-two churches in Manchester and Salford only eight were under the direction of the Church committee. While the area had increased, the actual work of the union had decreased. Church after church and school after school had been added to the town, but not to the union. In a word, a Church committee existed bearing a title which would seem to imply that they were concerned with the schools of the whole district, while in fact they were only interested in but a small section of them. It became clearly apparent that this state of things could not continue.

In 1837, Canon Mc.Grath, then Henry Walter Mc.Grath, a young man of unquestioned ability, came to St. Ann's. He quickly concentrated all the wealth and influence of the town

---

* We may assume that in a year or two the children will meet in Albert Square. St. Ann's Square is obviously too confined for the needs of the present day.

within its walls. He crowded the edifice with worshippers from every quarter of the town. His discourses were thoughtful, and his eloquence was of that nervous character which always attracts. Almost immediately after his institution as rector, Mr. Mc.Grath, and with him his churchwarden, Mr. Joynson, dissociated St. Ann's from the union. Both saw that as it existed the Church committee was not what it seemed to be. This and other circumstances brought the union to an end. On the 26th December, 1839, the committee held its last meeting. Having paid its debts, disposed of its property, and expressed its latest wishes, it practically proceeded to lay out its own body for decent interment, and then expired. Thus ended a union which, in its life of fifty-five years, had, as a single institution, done more for Manchester than has ever been done for it before or since.

From that day there has been no associate committee of Manchester Schools. Each school has acted independently, having a strictly parochial committee to undertake the charge of its interests. There have been unquestioned advantages in this. Nevertheless there have been disadvantages. While churches, or clergy, are by one tie or another banded together, our schools, one of the most important adjuncts of parochial work, have become separate entities—strangers to, if not estranged from, their neighbouring fellows. To this want of something more than nominal connection, we doubtless owe some of the evils that have of late years crept into the system. That which separately they have failed to cure, might easily have been expurgated by united action.

To a certain extent a remedy is now being applied, the merit of having discovered which belongs, I believe, to the dean.[*] Our schools are being banded together according to

* I must modify this statement to a certain extent. I believe Canon Birley, the Rev. J. N. Pocklington, and other clergymen have for many years urged some such principle of union.

the ruri-decanal boundaries. A committee is formed, of which the rural dean is chairman, and the clergy and superintendents of the several schools are the body. Examinations are held once every year for both teachers and scholars. Subjects taken from the Prayer Book and the Bible are given beforehand, and prizes are awarded to those who have acquitted themselves best. This is as it should be. The day for general committees, who should take cognizance of such strictly parochial matters as income and expenditure, is passed away. But a union based upon mutual sympathy, mutual interest, and mutual improvement can never be unnecessary, and ought never to be permitted to lapse.

Objections to the Sunday School system have been raised from the first. There has been a fear that parents might be encouraged to neglect their own more proper duties, and allow the school to undertake the responsibilities of home. There has been a fear that, although we speak of Church Schools, the Church might have to give place to the Schools; and that, instead of leading the child from home to the school, and from school to church, the adopters of this scheme might be contented with the first stage, and learn to depreciate the services of the Sanctuary. Others have feared that church catechising would become an obsolete custom, and the duties of godfather and godmother forgotten. Some of these evils have occurred. The catechism has not been made sufficiently prominent as a channel of instruction. Parents and godparents have undoubtedly in too many instances burdened the schoolroom with the responsibilities of the home and the font. But against these things we could bring a long array of advantages. This is not the place for arguing the matter. I will, however, ask one question. How has it fared with the rite of confirmation since the introduction of the Sunday School? How has it fared in Manchester? The number of candidates is beyond all proportion greater than that of former days; and what is still more important, a greater care has been exercised in the preparation of the children for that solemn ordinance. The teacher's work has re-acted upon the clergyman. He has been absolutely compelled to make more of the season of instruction than had hitherto been customary. The Rev. John Clayton, of the Sacred Trinity in Salford, some thirty years before the institution of Sunday Schools, brought before the Bishop seventy people for confirmation, all over fifty years of age. This spoke much for Mr. Clayton's individual labours; but it spoke volumes against the negligence and apathy of that time. Could anything like this by any possibility happen now? It could not, and we claim Sunday Schools to be the main, if not entire reason.

Another objection has been raised more recently. It is alleged that our Sunday Schools have become "mere courting institutions." This is at once true and false. That they are "mere" trysting places for purposes of courtship needs no contradiction. That many, very many alliances are there formed which culminate in wedlock is undeniable. I look upon this as a distinct advantage. The subject is a delicate one ; but it has been raised, and I would speak delicately. I do not quote my own view, but that of many clergymen older, and wiser, and more competent to give a judgment than myself, when I assert that upon wedlock our Sunday Schools have unintentionally exercised a most wholesome effect. On occasions of festivity a most thorough watchfulness on the part of ministers and teachers is only too often required ; but they can point to numberless marriages happily consummated, both among teachers and scholars, the direct result of friendships formed at the Sunday School. There are a hundred opportunities for our elder scholars to form acquaintance with unworthy companions. Here is one where the two are connected by associations that are all hallowed. It is so strong that they will attend the school after they are married and have children of their own. And the one thought of both is that those children may, at such an age as is convenient, be nurtured in the same school, and under the same influences as themselves. Evils attach to this unintended, and still unintended result. But the evil is overbalanced by the good. Against the mischief it lies with the clergyman and his teachers to do battle. Here the command to "watch" is most obligatory.

One more thought and I conclude. It is to our Sunday Schools we owe a large amount of literature suited to the capacity of children. I do not refer to the teachers, who in teaching others have learnt to require a literature for themselves. I do not refer to lending libraries, by which pure books have been introduced to the parents of the scholars. I speak simply of our hymnology. Dr. Watts did much for children, but it was left to our Sunday Schools to collect a body of songs and hymns for the use of the youth of the country, which no other land possesses. Even the anniversary, with its local attempts at religious rhyming, has been beneficial. Who will not be thankful for an institution which brought Canon Stowell's exquisite hymns into existence ? Some of them, written hurriedly, will die ; some will live for ever. I might speak of "Jesus is our Shepherd," sung by every school in the North. I would speak only of a hymn, than which there is not one in the English language more sweetly devotional. It deserves even more praise than Mr. Bickersteth has awarded it.

> From every stormy wind that blows,
> From every swelling tide of woes,
> There is a calm, a sure retreat :
> 'Tis found beneath the mercy-seat.

> There is a place where Jesus sheds,
> The oil of gladness on our heads :
> A place than all beside more sweet :
> It is the blood-stain'd mercy-seat.

There is a spot where spirits blend,
And friend holds fellowship with friend :
Though sundered far, by faith they meet
Around one common mercy-seat.

Ah, whither could we flee for aid,
When tempted, desolate, dismay'd ?
Or how the hosts of hell defeat,
Had suffering saints no mercy-seat ?

There, there on eagle wing we soar,
And time and sense seem all no more,
And heaven comes down our souls to greet,
And glory crowns the mercy-seat.

Poetically the last verse somewhat suffers by comparison with the rest. But we may hope that all future compilers of hymn books will refrain from trying to "improve" it. We have had too many hymns spoilt already by jobbers in hymn-ology. Especially, at least, would we ask them to leave in its integrity this hallowed outcome of the Manchester and Salford Sunday School system.

"An Act for building a Church or Chapel in the Town of
" Manchester, in the County of Lancaster.

" PREAMBLE—

" WHEREAS, the Parish of Manchester, in the County
of Lancaster, is of a large extent, and very populous,
and hath only one Church (which is Collegiate, and Incorporated
by the name of the Warden and Fellows of Christ Colledge, in
Manchester, founded by King Charles the First), and some
Chapels of Ease in it, which are not large enough to contain
the third part of the Inhabitants for the commodious performing and hearing divine service : And whereas divers well-
disposed persons, inhabitants of the said parish, and others,
with the consent and approbation as well of the Queen's most
excellent Majesty (who is patroness thereof in right of the
Dutchy of Lancaster) as of the Warden and Fellows of the
said Church (who in their Corporate Capacity are incumbents
thereof), as also of the Bishop of the Diocese of Chester,
wherein the same lies, are willing and desirous at their own
expences and charges to erect a new Church there, so as the
advowson or Patronage thereof may be vested in the same
Bishop of Chester, and his successors, in manner hereinafter
mentioned, which cannot be done without Act of Parliament :
And whereas William Baguley, of Kirsley, in the said County

of Lancaster, Gentleman, is seized to him and his heirs of a certain field or close adjoining to the town of Manchester, called 'The Acres,' wherein a Fair is yearly held, belonging to the Manor of Manchester, called Acres Fair, and is willing to allow and give three score yards in length and forty yards in breadth, about the middle of the South side of the said Close, to be inclosed for a churchyard and for the building of a Church therein, together with such ways to the same as are hereinafter mentioned. And whereas Sir John Bland, baronet, and Dame Ann his wife, to whom the said Manor of Manchester does at present belong, in Right of the said Dame Ann Bland for her life, and Oswald Mosley, junior, Esquire, John Thornhagh, Esquire, and Oswald Mosley, senior, Esquire, to whom the remainders and reversion of the said Manor after the death of the said Dame Ann Bland do belong, for promoting the said pious work, and in consideration of the said William Baguley giving the said ground to be inclosed for a Churchyard as aforesaid, are content and willing that the said fair should be extinguished, and the said Close discharged thereof (except as hereinafter mentioned) : Be it therefore enacted by the Queen's Most Excellent Majesty, by and with the advice and consent of the Lords Spiritual and Temporal and Commons in this present Parliament assembled, and by the authority of the same—That it shall and may be lawful to and for the Inhabitants of the said parish and others, that shall be willing voluntarily to contribute to the same at their own costs and charges to inclose with a wall the said piece of ground of three score yards in length and forty yards in breadth allotted, or that shall be allotted by the said William Baguley, in the said Close called 'The Acres,' for a Churchyard, and thereupon or within the same to erect and build a New Church, to be consecrated and used for the public worship of God, and Instruction of the inhabitants of the said Parish of Manchester in the true Religion now professed in the Church of England as by Law

Established : And that the said ground so to be inclosed for a Churchyard, and the Church to be therein or thereupon erected shall from and after the consecration thereof be and be taken for the new Church and yard meant and intended by this Act.

"And be it further enacted by the authority aforesaid, that the Patronage, Advowson, Free Disposition, and Right of Collator, Nominator, and Donator of and to the Bishop of Chester to be said new Church, when and as soon as the same Patron. shall be erected and consecrated, shall Appertain unto, and are hereby vested in the Lord Bishop of Chester for the time being, and his Successors for ever. And that from and after the said Lord Bishop or his successors shall have collated or nominated any incumbent to the said Church, the said incumbent shall be and is hereby from thenceforth incorporated, and shall have perpetual succession by the name Incumbent of Rector of St. Ann's Church, in Manchester, and Incorporated, that the Freehold and Inheritance of the said new etc. Church and Church-yard shall, from thenceforth, Appertain to, and the same are hereby from thenceforth vested in the said Incumbent and his successors for ever in the same manner as the Freehold and Inheritance of a Parish Church is by the laws of this Realm vested in the Incumbent thereof. And the said incumbent and his successors are hereby enabled and made capable from thenceforth to take and accept any grant or grants of any other convenient or necessary way or ways to the said new Church, besides the ways or streets particularly mentioned in this Act, which other way or ways (if the Grantor or Grantors think fit) shall be also free and open for the use of the said fair to be held in the said ways or streets hereinafter mentioned, and for such other purposes as shall be specified in such grant or grants.

"And be it further enacted by the Authority aforesaid, That the said Incumbent, so to be collated or nominated, and his successors, shall be entitled unto the Benefit and advantage of all Pews and Seats in the said New Church, which shall from time to time be let and set by the Incumbent of the said New Church for the Time being, with the consent of six or more Inhabitants of the said Parish, to be from time to time commissioned by the said Bishop, and his successors, by Deed or Deeds for any number of years not exceeding One and Twenty years; and the said Incumbent and his successors are hereby enabled to sue for such rents as shall be reserved by such Deed or Deeds, and in such Courts and places as Parsons of Parishes may sue for their Tythes, provided, nevertheless, that nothing herein contained shall be or extend, or be construed, or taken to be, or extend to the prejudice, Loss, or Diminution of any of the Rights, Dues, or Privileges of, or belonging to the said Warden, or Fellows and their successors, of or belonging to the Chaplains of the said Collegiate Church, or to the Clerks or Sextons of the said Parish Church, for the time being. But that all Fees, Dues, Rights, Privileges, and Perquisites, usually enjoyed by, paid, and of Rights belonging to the said Warden and Fellows, the said Chaplains, Parish Clerks, and Sextons respectively, and their respective successors, for Weddings, Christenings, Churchings, and Burials, and on all or any other Accounts whatsoever, and all Suits, Actions, and Remedies for the same (except only what is otherwise Ordered or Provided for by this Act) be reserved, Continued, and remain Due and Payable to, and Recoverable by them and each of them respectively, and their and each of their respective successors, as fully and amply to all Intents and Purposes as if this Act had not been made.

" Provided always, that to the end and Intent the said new Church may be kept and preserved more clean and decent, No graves to there shall be no Graves or Burying places made be in the body or allowed within the Body of the said new Church, of the church. but only in the said new Churchyard to be enclosed and Consecrated as aforesaid, And that all Christenings and

Weddings to be had and solemnized in the said New Church, and all Burials in the said New Church yard shall be registered as usual in the Register of the said Collegiate Church.

" And to the intent and purpose that the Sacraments of Baptism and the Lord's Supper may be duly and rightly Administered in the said new Church and Bread and Wine be provided for the holy Eucharist there, and the said New Church and its Utensils and Ornaments and the said New Church yard may be well and Carefully repaired and Looked after and Kept clean and safe,

" Be it further Enacted by the Authority aforesaid, That it shall and may be lawful to and for the said Bishop and his successors yearly and every year to nominate and Appoint One or more Church Wardens for the said Purposes, who shall be subject to the visitation of the said Bishop and his successors, and shall be sworn to Execute the said office, and to appear and make Presentments at the said Bishop's visitation, and at the Courts of the Rural Dean of the Deanery of Manchester in such manner as hath been usual in other Churches of the said Deanery : And that the said Church Warden or Church Wardens shall, and is, and are hereby, after he or they shall be nominated as aforesaid, Incorporated and Enabled to Take and purchase to them and their Successors, Lands, Tenements, Rents, or Hereditaments, not exceeding the value of Fifty Pounds per annum, to be employed and Disposed of for finding Bread and Wine for the Holy Eucharist, and for Repairing and Beautifying the said new church, and for providing Utensils and Ornaments for the same, and for Looking after the same and Keeping the same clean and safe, and for other necessary Uses and Purposes, relating to, and on account of the said new church and its church yard.

(margin note: Bishop of Chester to appoint Church Wardens, &c.)

" And be it further enacted by the Authority aforesaid, that the said Fair called Acres Fair from and after the

K

Erecting and Consecrating the said New Church shall be, and
the same is hereby from thenceforth Extinguished;
and the said Close thereof for ever discharged
(save and except only in the Ways or Streets hereinafter mentioned) he the said William Baguley,
his Heirs, and Assigns making and leaving such Ways or
Streets as are hereinafter mentioned.

Acres Fair extinguished, save in the ways after mentioned.

" And be it further enacted by the Authority aforesaid, that
it shall and may be lawful to and for the said William Baguley,
his Heirs, and Assigns to Erect any Messuages or
Buildings, or to enclose Gardens, Courts, Yards,
and Backsides upon in and out of the said Close
or any part thereof, or otherwise to Use or Improve
the same at his pleasure (except the said piece of
Ground to be enclosed for the said New Church and Churchyard, and the said Ways or Streets hereinafter mentioned); and
that all the said Close, as well as the said Ground, to be
enclosed for the said New Church and Churchyard, as all the
rest and residue thereof (Except the said intended Ways or
Streets), shall be for ever held and enjoyed by the said William
Baguley, his Heirs, or Assigns, making or leaving such Streets
or Ways as are hereinafter described and mentioned.

William Baguley may Erect Buildings, &c., in the Close, &c.

"And be it further enacted by the Authority aforesaid, That
the said William Baguley, his Heirs and Assigns, shall make
and leave a way or street from the north side
of the said Close called "The Acres" straight
and directly up to the said Church yard, of Thirty
Yards Broad at the least, and also one other Street or Way of
Eight Yards Broad at the least, quite cross the said Close from
the East side thereof up by the North side of the said New
Church Yard, to the West side of the said Close and so on
from thence to the way hereinafter mentioned, now to belong
to the said William Baguley, and also one other way or Street
of Five Yards Broad at the least, quite cross the North side of

And make a Church Way, &c.

the said Close, and Two other ways, each of Five yards broad at the least, and on the East side of the said Close, leading from the said last mentioned cross way, on the North side thereof unto the said other cross way hereinbefore mentioned and intended to be Eight Yards Broad and the other on the West side of the said Close leading from the said Cross way on the North side thereof unto the said other Cross way intended to be Eight Yards Broad.

"And be it further enacted by the Authority, aforesaid, That the said Streets or Ways of Thirty Yards Broad, and The Streets Eight Yards Broad, also one other way which doth shall be free now belong to the said William Baguley, and he and open as now hath or is Entitled unto leading from a Street Common Highways. in the said town of Manchester, called Deansgate, into the said Close, called 'The Acres' shall be for ever from and after the Consecration of the said new Church, free and open as common highways, to all persons whatsoever, with Coaches, Carts, Carriages, and outherwise, and for their horses and cattle for the use of the said new Church and Church Yard, and Fair to be held and kept in the Ways and Streets aforesaid, and for all other Purposes, and on all other occasions whatsoever, and at all Times and Seasons, at their free will and pleasure.

"Provided always, and it is hereby declared, and enacted, That it shall and may be lawful to and for the Owners of the Owners of the Manor of Manchester for the time being, for ever Manor of to hold and Keep a Fair in all or any the said Manchester Ways or Streets at the Time and in such manner as may hold a Fair in the the said Fair, called Acres Fair, hath been usually ways and kept, and that the said Fair shall from and after means. the Consecration of the said new Church appertain to and go allong with the said Manor of Manchester in such Plight, Manner, and Condition, as the said former Fair did appertain to and go allong with the same, and that the Owner and Owners of the said Manor shall from thenceforth for ever have and enjoy such tolls and Duties as belonging to and on Account of the said Fair, to be held in the said streets or ways as before this Act did of Right belong to the said Former Fair, and shall have like Actions and Remedies for the same, yet so as not to charge any Person or Persons with any more or other, or greater Tolls or Duties than did of Right belong to the said former Fair.

"Provided further, That in Case any New or other Fair or Fairs, Market or Markets shall at any time or times hereafter be held and kept upon any part or parts of the said Close called 'The Acres,' the Tolls and Duties thereto belonging or to arise upon Account of the same, shall go to and be received by the Owner and Owners for the time being of the said Manor of Manchester.

Owners shall have the Tolls of any New Fairs.

"Saving to the Queen's Most Excellent Majesty, her Heirs and Successors (otherwise than as the Patrons of the said Collegiate or Parish Church of Manchester), and to all and every other Person and Persons, Bodies Politick and Corporate, their Heirs and Successors, Executors and Administrators (other than and except the said Warden and Fellows and their Successors, and also the said William Baguley and his Heirs, Sir John Bland and Dame Ann his Wife, Oswald Mosley, junior; John Thornhagh, John White, Saint Andrew Thornhagh, and Oswald Mosley, senior; and the Sons and Daughters of them each or any of them, whether already born or hereafter to be born, and their and each or any of their Heirs, Executors, and Administrators; and the Heirs Male and Heirs Female and Heirs of the Bodies of them every or any of them, and of all or any of the Sons and Daughters of them or any of them; and all Persons entrusted for them or any of them, their Heirs, Executors, and Administrators), all such Right, Title, and Interest, as they every or any of them would have had in case this Act had not been made."

Saving Clause.

Appendix II.

Report of the State of the Sunday Schools in the Towns of
Manchester and Salford Belonging to the Established
Church, from 1st July, 1809, to 1st July, 1810.

TO THE PUBLIC.

I T is at this day generally acknowledged that there is no duty of greater importance to religion, and to the good order of society in general, than the careful education of children.   And there is hardly anything which requires a more prudent and constant application of our best care and attention.

The simple plan of education adopted in these schools is to familiarise the mind to the love of truth, to open to the eye the genuine source of moral obligation in the will of the Creator, and to blend religion with the very heart ; to plant, in short, the virtuous purpose in the soul, to protect and foster its growth with the dews of Heaven till it rises to yield its fruits before the throne of God.

In the present state of society few have the leisure and capacity of forming and improving the minds of youth.   The time of the labourer, the husbandman, and the mechanic, who constitute the majority of the people, is fully occupied with the necessities of their families.   Are they, then, at once to feel the exaction and the incapacity of a duty, to lament the advantage of enlightened society existing in no degree for them, to behold poverty and ignorance mutually acquiring, from their fatal union, growth, vigour, and stability ?   No ; with the other wants of the poor, the trust of their education is committed to the charity of the rich by that Being who ordains various conditions to be the means of various duties, and in the necessities of one supplies the opportunity and exercise of benevolence to another.

Now no scheme could be more conducive to instruct the poor in the knowledge of their God and Saviour, than the establishment of Sunday schools. The Sabbath day is dedicated to that most excellent purpose, when they are initiated into that kind of knowledge which is best adapted to their station in life.

If, therefore, the children of the poor are preserved from idleness and dissipation, and directed to those paths which lead to honesty and labour, if they are rescued from the snares of the devil and made true disciples of Jesus Christ, if they are induced to love God, to honour His holy name, and to follow the precepts of that religion which animates us to a holy course of living, and thus prepares us for the enjoyment of eternal happiness in the future life, we must ever admire the wisdom and design of Sunday schools.

It is impossible, in the limits prescribed for an address of this kind, to say all that might be said upon so very excellent an institution : Suffice it to observe, that an experience of near thirty years has sufficiently shewn, to its most zealous friends and supporters, its intrinsic value, notwithstanding all the objections which have been urged against it.

OFFICERS FOR THE ENSUING YEAR.

The Rev. T. BLACKBURN, LL.D., Warden of the Collegiate Church, President.

Vice-Presidents.

HENRY BARTON, Esq.	WILLIAM COOPER, Esq.
GEORGE WALKER, Esq.	Mr. THOS. WHITELEGG,
WILLIAM FOX, Esq.	Mr. N. GOULD.

Mr. SAMUEL MOTTRAM, Treasurer.
Rev. EBENEZER BOOTH, Secretary.
Mr. N. GOULD and Mr. T. O. GILL, Auditors.
Mr. N. SHELMERDINE, Librarian.

Committee.

The acting Magistrates of the Division of Manchester, the Boroughreeve and Constables of Manchester and Salford for the time being, together with the Clergy of the under-named churches, and the Annual Subscribers of one guinea each.

COLLEGIATE CHURCH,	ST. JAMES'S,
ST. ANN'S,	ST. MICHAEL'S,
ST. MARY'S,	ST. PETER'S,
ST. PAUL'S,	TRINITY, and ⎱ Salford.
ST. JOHN'S,	ST. STEPHEN'S, ⎰

Subscriptions are received by the President, Vice-Presidents, Treasurer, and Secretary at any time, by whom all benefactions will be gratefully received.

RECEIPTS.				PAYMENTS.			
	£	s.	d.		£	s.	d.
Balance in hand	330	8	5	Teachers' Salaries, Rents, Coals, Candles, &c.	786	2	3
Collected in the Churches	383	9	6	Joiner's and other Bills for Sundry Repairs	244	1	7
Subscribed in the Districts	610	7	9	Books, Stationary, Advertising, &c.	234	2	2
Anniversary Sermon	61	16	8	Balance of Interest	19	19	4
				Balance, 1st July, 1810	101	17	0

6th March, 1811.
Audited { NATHL. GOULD.
by us, { T. O. GILL.   £1386 2 4   £1386 2 4

It is highly necessary to observe that through repeated delays in effecting the collections, the reports, which have uniformly been made up each year to the 1st July, have been delayed long past that time. This not only occasions a considerable loss to the establishment in interest, but also gives these accounts the appearance of being in a better state than is really the case ; in proof of which it may be proper to observe that none of the subscriptions in this account, to the amount of £610. 7s. 9d., which have the appearance of having been received before the 1st July, 1810, had then come in, therefore, instead of the treasurer having then a balance in his hands, he was greatly in advance to the charity. It is nevertheless deemed proper to persevere in this mode of stating the accounts lest a year's subscriptions be eventually lost ; and it is earnestly hoped this consideration will operate as a powerful motive with the gentlemen who kindly undertake to collect the subscriptions to use their best endeavours to complete the same as early as possible, so that by gaining a month or two each year the report may, ere long, be not *merely dated* but *made out* on the 1st July, and all the subscriptions then paid up.

In order to shew the progressive state of this establishment an account is here given of the receipts and payments for the last six years, together with the number of scholars each year,* whence it appears that the schools have increased in a much greater ratio than the contributions. And it is the opinion of those who are best acquainted with the schools that of late great improvements have been made in the conducting of many of them, and that in consequence the scholars are much more regular in their attendance, and make greater improvement both in their learning and general conduct. On account of the increase in the number of scholars, and the taking and furnishing larger schools for their accommodation in some of the districts, the expences of the establishment have this year greatly exceeded its income, and consequently its funds are in a very depressed state. This, whilst it calls for the utmost œconomy on the part of the conductors of the charity, will, it is hoped, induce that further support from a generous public which it stands in need of.

* See pages 130 and 131.

SUBSCRIPTIONS.

A

	£	s.	d.
R. J. D. Ashworth	3	3	.0
Miss Alexander	2	2	0
Mr. James Ackers.............	1	1	0
Mr. Robert Appleby.........	1	1	0
Mr. Robert Andrew	1	1	0
Mr. William Asheton	1	1	0
Mr. Richard Alsop	1	1	0
Messrs. John Aspinwall &			
Co.	1	1	0
Mr. Alsop	1	1	0
Mr. Samuel Aaron	1	0	0
Mr. Robert Atkinson	0	10	6
Mr. John Austin	0	10	6
Mr. Thomas Aldcroft	0	10	6
Messrs. Amies and Dale ...	0	10	6
M. James Andrew............	0	10	6
Mr. J. Armstrong	0	10	6
Messrs. Thos. Andrew &			
Son	0	10	6
Mr. John Ainscow............	0	10	6
Mr. John Amies	0	10	6
Mr. Thomas Astley	0	10	6
Mr. Samuel Arrowsmith ...	0	10	6
Mr. John Atkinson	0	10	6
Mr. James Andrew, sen. ...	0	10	6
Mr. Ellis Aspinall............	0	10	0
Mr. James Appleton.........	0	7	0
Mr. Richard Alsop	0	6	0
Mr. James Aspell	0	5	0
Mr. Philip Antrobuss	0	5	0
Mr. William Aspell	0	5	0
Mr. Richard Acton	0	5	0

	£	s.	d.
Mr. Thomas Appleton	0	5	0
Mr. Peter Abraham	0	5	0
Mr. John Adamthwaite......	0	5	0
Mr. Thomas Alderson	0	5	0
Mr. Robert Ashley	0	5	0

B

	£	s.	d.
Rev. T. Blackburn, LL.D..	2	2	0
Mr. Richard Barlow..........	2	2	0
Messrs. H. & W. Burgess ..	2	2	0
Mr. Henry Barton.............	2	2	0
Rev. E. Booth	1	1	0
Miss Jane Norton Bailey ...	1	1	0
Miss Byrom	1	1	0
Mr. Michael Bentley, Esq..	1	1	0
Mr. John Bousfield	1	1	0
Messrs. J. & G. Bennet ...	1	1	0
Mess. Borradaile & Atkinson	1	1	0
Mr. John Bury	1	1	0
Mr. George Beatty	1	1	0
Mr. James Bailey	1	1	0
Mr. Thomas Boardman......	1	1	0
Mr. John Bill...	1	1	0
Mr. Thomas Blackwell......	1	1	0
Mr. Samuel Buxton	1	1	0
Mr. James Brownhill	1	1	0
Mr. Samuel Bradshaw	1	1	0
Mr. Thomas Borron	1	1	0
Mr. William Byfield	1	1	0
Mr. Buckley	1	1	0
Messrs. H. Barton & Co....	1	1	0
Mr. Joseph Benton	1	1	0

	£	s.	d.
Mr. James Bateman	1	1	0
Messrs. Bateman & Co.	1	1	0
Mrs. Mary Basnett	1	1	0
Mr. James Bateman, sen.	1	1	0
Mr. James Bateman, jun.	1	1	0
Mr. James Bradford	1	0	0
Messrs. J. & J. Barker	1	0	0
Messrs. Benton & Smith	1	0	0
Mrs. Bradock	1	0	0
Mr. Joseph Benton	1	0	0
Mr. Richard Bassel	0	14	0
A. B.	0	10	6
Mr. William Brett	0	10	6
Mr. F. Brenand	0	10	0
Mr. John Bell	0	10	6
Mr. William Burton	0	10	6
Mr. John Barlow	0	10	0
Mr. Morton Bunting	0	10	6
Mr. William Bowman	0	10	0
Mr. Henry Barrowclough	0	10	6
Mr. Samuel Brett	0	10	6
Mr. James Brereton	0	10	6
Mr. Joseph Ball	0	10	6
Mr. John Bridgeford	0	10	6
Mrs. Jane Burgess	0	10	6
Mr. Beverley	0	10	6
Mr. George Blore	0	10	6
Mr. Richard Bowman	0	10	6
Mr. Anthony Bennet	0	10	6
Mrs. Margaret Burton	0	10	6
Mr. John Braithwaite	0	10	6
Mr. Robert Broadhead	0	10	6
Mr. William Bowker	0	10	6
Mr. John Barlow	0	10	6
Mr. John Boardman	0	10	6
Mr. Henry Bond	0	10	6
Mr. Thomas Bennet	0	10	6
Mr. James Braddock	0	10	6
Mr. John Brown	0	10	6
Mr. George Backhouse	0	10	6

	£	s.	d.
Mr. Benjamin Binyon	0	10	6
Messrs. Burton and Co.	0	10	6
Messrs. S. & J. Briddon	0	10	6
Messrs. Bowers & Lockwood	0	10	6
Mr. John Bell	0	10	6
Mr. Thomas Bird	0	10	6
Mr. Peter Bayley	0	10	6
Mr. William Barker	0	10	6
Messrs. Brennands & Co.	0	10	6
Mr. David Bellhouse	0	10	6
Doctor Bardsley	0	10	6
Mr. Bowman	0	10	6
Mr. Brown	0	10	6
Mr. Samuel Birch	0	10	6
Mr. Thomas Brownbill	0	10	6
Messrs. T. & D. Bancroft	0	10	6
Mr. Henry Bowman	0	10	6
Mr. James Barnes	0	10	6
Messrs. Boden & Winder	0	10	6
Mr. Thomas Bagshaw	0	10	0
Messrs. Burn & Campbell	0	7	0
Mr. Thomas Brotherton	0	7	0
Mr. Thomas Berry	0	7	0
Mr. William Briddon	0	7	0
Mr. Joseph Barton	0	7	0
Mr. Thomas Bibby	0	7	0
Mr. John Burgess	0	7	0
Mr. Henry Bellot	0	7	0
Mr. James Brown	0	7	0
Mr. Thomas Beal	0	7	0
Mr. Joseph Brown	0	7	0
Mr. James Bloomley	0	7	0
Mr. John Bromley	0	5	0
Mr. John Boden	0	5	0
Mr. Thomas Beaver	0	5	0
Mr. Thomas Brough	0	5	0
Mr. James Barrett	0	5	0
Mr. Thomas Boothman	0	5	0
Mrs. Rachael Butterworth	0	5	0
Mr. Heally Barker	0	5	0

	£	s.	d.
Mr. John Beaumont	0	5	0
Mr. John Boothman	0	5	0
Mr. John Barnet	0	5	0
Mr. Samuel Booth	0	5	0
Mr. Samuel Borough	0	5	0
Mr. William Ballans	0	5	0
Mr. John Bingham	0	5	0
Mr. John Becton	0	5	0
Mr. William Bradley	0	5	0
Mrs. Mary Bradshaw	0	5	0
Mr. Stock Brown	0	5	0
Mr. Bramhall	0	5	0
Mr. John Bancroft	0	5	0
Mr. John Broffitt	0	5	0
Mr. John Blinkhorn	0	5	0
Mr. John Baggs	0	5	0
Mr. William Bowker	0	5	0
Mr. John Bradley	0	5	0

C

Rev. John Clowes, M.A.	2	2	0
Mr. William Cowper, sen.	2	2	0
Messrs. Claytons	2	2	0
Mr. Edward Chantler	2	0	0
Mr. Richard Cundall	1	1	0
Mr. James Chapman	1	1	0
Messrs. John Close & Co.	1	1	0
Mr. James Cooke	1	1	0
Mr. John Clegg	1	1	0
Mr. John Collier	1	1	0
Messrs. Thomas Coates & Co.	1	1	0
Messrs. Thos. Cardwell & Co.	1	1	0
Mr. Richard Clogg	1	1	0
Mr. Robert Chadwick	1	1	0
Mr. William Clowes	1	1	0
Mr. William Cowdroy	1	1	0
Mrs. Ann Crompton	1	1	0
Mr. John Craig	1	1	0
Mr. Edmund Clegg	1	1	0
Messrs. Crallan & Shaw	1	1	0

	£	s.	d.
Mr. H. Cardwell	1	1	0
Mr. John Clough	0	10	6
Mr. Archibald Caruthers	0	10	6
Mrs. Elizabeth Chapman	0	10	6
Messrs. S. Cooke & Co.	0	10	6
Mrs. Crompton	0	10	6
Mr. William Cowper	0	10	6
Messrs. Crewdson & Co.	0	10	6
Mr. William Cowdroy	0	10	6
Mr. John Cowper	0	10	6
Mr. John Clegg	0	10	6
Mr. Thomas Challender	0	10	6
Mr. Crompton	0	10	6
Mr. Thomas Calvert	0	10	6
Mr. Matthew Corbett	0	10	6
Mr. John Cockbaine	0	10	6
Mr. John Curtis	0	10	6
Mr. John Crowther	0	10	6
Mr. John Chadwick	0	10	6
Mr. E. Chesshyre	0	10	6
Mr. G. R. Crompton	0	10	6
Mr. Allen Carr	0	10	6
Mr. Bold Cooke	0	10	6
Mr. Martin Clayton	0	7	0
Mr. John Clarkson	0	7	0
Mr. Peter Collier	0	7	0
Mr. Peter Coe	0	5	0
Mr. Joseph Collier	0	5	0
Mrs. Campbell	0	5	0
Mr. Thomas Cantrell	0	5	0
Mr. A. Cowen	0	5	0
Mr. David Campbell	0	5	0
Mr. Brian Coulthard	0	5	0
Mr. Carr	0	5	0
Mr. Samuel Crosbie	0	5	0
Mr. Samuel Cheetham	0	5	0
Mr. Edward Cornes	0	5	0
Mr. James Cheetham	0	5	0
Messrs. Clarkes	0	5	0
Mr. Peter Cluney	0	5	0

	£	s.	d.
Mr. Thomas Chesshire	o	5	o
Mr. Caygill	o	5	o

D

	£	s.	d.
Mr. Micheal Dalton	1	1	o
Messrs. T. & J. Dawson	1	1	o
Mr. Jacob Davis	1	1	o
Messrs. T. & J. Drinkwater	1	1	o
Messrs. R. & W. Dean	1	1	o
Miss Doxon	1	1	o
Mr. John Dawson	1	1	o
Mr. Thomas Darewell	1	1	o
Mr. William Dunstan	1	o	o
Mr. John Duckett	o	10	6
Mr. Francis Dixon	o	10	6
Mr. Thomas Deny	o	10	6
Mr. J. Dorrington	o	10	6
Mr. George Downes	o	10	6
Mr. Joseph Docker	o	10	6
Mr. Joseph Dakeyne	o	10	6
Mr. Samuel Davis	o	10	6
Mr. James Dean	o	7	o
Mr. James Denton	o	7	o
Mr. Charles Davenport	o	7	o
Mr. Davenport	o	7	o
Mr. Thomas Dickinson	o	5	o
Mr. Samuel Dearden	o	5	o

E

	£	s.	d.
Mr. Ellam	1	o	o
Mr. Charles Ellenthorpe	o	10	6
Miss Ellenthorpe	o	10	6
Mr. Ralph Ellam	o	10	6
Mr. Isaac Edge	o	10	6
Mr. John Eastham	o	10	6
Mr. William Eccles	o	10	6
Mr. Richard Eglington	o	10	6
Mr. Edward Evans	o	10	o
Mr. James Evans	o	10	6
Mr. Eaton	o	7	o

	£	s.	d.
Mrs. Evans	o	7	o
Mr. Richard Elliot	o	5	o

F

	£	s.	d.
William Fox, Esq.	2	2	o
Mr. Peter Fletchter	1	1	o
Mr. T. S. Fogg	1	1	o
Mess. Fogg, Birch & Hampson	1	1	o
A Friend	1	o	o
A Friend	1	o	o
Mr. John Fullarton	o	10	6
Mrs. Ann Ford & Sons	o	10	6
A Friend	o	10	6
Miss Foster	o	10	6
Mr. Edward Frazer	o	10	6
Mr. William Fell	o	10	6
Mr. Edward Foden	o	10	6
Mr. John Foxlow	o	10	6
Mr. Thomas Foster	o	10	6
Mr. James Fielding	o	10	6
Mr. Joseph Fletcher	o	10	6
Mr. James Fisher	o	10	6
Messrs. Fawcett and Sade..	o	10	6
Mr. Archibald Fullerton	o	10	6
Mr. Richard Fitton	o	10	6
A Friend	o	10	6
Mr. Furness	o	10	6
Mr. John Froggat	o	10	6
Mr. Joseph Finn	o	10	6
Mrs. Nancy Fisher	o	10	6
Mr. Thomas Fleming	o	10	6
Mr. T. W. Faulkner	o	8	o
A Friend	o	7	o
Mr. Thomas Fildes	o	5	o
Mr. James Foster	o	5	o
Mr. Fell	o	5	o
Mr. John Fletcher	o	5	o
A Friend	o	5	o
A Friend	o	5	o

	£	s.	d.
Mr. Fletcher	o	5	o
Mr. James France	o	5	o
A Friend	o	5	o

G

	£	s.	d.
N. Gould, Esq.	5	5	o
Mr. George Gould	1	1	o
Sir Robert Gore Booth	1	1	o
Mr. Joseph Grave	1	1	o
Mr. James Gordon	1	1	o
Mr. Joseph Gould	1	1	o
Mr. Joseph Gleave	1	1	o
Mr. Edward Garrett	1	1	o
Mr. Thomas Goulbourn	1	1	o
Mr. James Gregory	1	1	o
Mr. B. H. Green	1	1	o
Mr. T. O. Gill	1	1	o
Mr. Francis Goadsby	1	1	o
Messrs. Gardner & Harter.	1	1	o
Mr. John Grant	1	o	o
Mrs. Grimshaw	o	10	6
Mr. John Golding	o	10	6
Mr. Thomas Grost	o	10	6
Mr. Jacob Goodier	o	10	6
Mr. J. Glover	o	10	6
Messrs. Gleave & Fallows..	o	10	6
Mrs. Ellen Griffiths	o	10	6
Mr. Robert Green	o	10	6
Alexander Glendenning	o	10	6
Mrs. Gorton	o	10	6
Mr. Thomas Goulbourn	o	10	6
Mr. Thomas Geary	o	10	6
Mr. Green	o	10	6
Mr. George Darewell	o	10	6
Mr. Benjamin Green	o	10	6
Mr. Thomas Grundy	o	10	6
Mr. John Gregory	o	10	6
Mrs. Gomersall	o	10	6
Mr. Reuben Gill	o	10	6
Mr. Benjamin Goodall	o	10	6

	£	s.	d.
Mr. William Goodall	o	10	6
Mr. Richard Greenwood	o	7	o
Mr. T. J. Green	o	7	o
Mr. John Gerrard	o	7	o
Mr. John Gregory	o	7	o
Mr. John Greenhalgh	o	5	o
Mr. Thomas Greenwood	o	5	o
Mr. John Grimshaw	o	5	o
Mr. Thomas Grace	o	5	o
Mr. John Greenhalgh	o	5	o
Mrs. A. Getty	o	5	o
Mr. John Gratrix	o	5	o
Mr. Thomas Gittins	o	5	o
Mr. Lawrence Gaskell	o	5	o

H

	£	s.	d.
Messrs. Hughes & Co.	1	1	o
Miss Hall	1	1	o
Mr. Thomas Hewes	1	1	o
Mr. Thomas Holdsworth	1	1	o
Mr. Samuel Hyde	1	1	o
Mr. Charles Hammond	1	1	o
Mr. Robert Howarth	1	1	o
Mr. William Hutchinson	1	1	o
Messrs. Robert Holt & Sons.	1	1	o
Mr. John Harrison	1	1	o
Miss Halls	1	1	o
Miss Heywood	1	1	o
Messrs. J. & G. Holford	1	1	o
Mr. Higginson	1	1	o
Mr. Richard Higginson	1	1	o
Messrs. Hughes and Co.	1	1	o
Mr. William Hyde	1	1	o
Mr. James Hall	1	1	o
Mrs. M. Horrocks	1	1	o
Mr. D. Hulme	1	1	o
Messrs. Holgate & Davies .	1	1	o
Mr. Thomas Hampson	1	1	o
Mr. W. Hallsworth	1	1	o
Mr. James Heywood	o	10	6

	£	s.	d.
Mr. Matthew Hedley	o	10	6
Mr. M. Holladay	o	10	6
Mr. John Heywood	o	10	6
Mr. Samuel Hurst	o	10	6
Mr. John Hogarth	o	10	6
Mr. John Holt	o	10	6
Mr. Ryal Holme	o	10	6
Mr. William Hankinson	o	10	6
Messrs. T. & E. Hope	o	10	6
Mrs. Ann Holford	o	10	6
Mr. F. M. Hodson	o	10	6
Mr. James Harrop	o	10	6
Mr. Halstead	o	10	6
Mr. Nathaniel Halliwell	o	10	6
Mr. James Heap	o	10	6
Miss Holland	o	10	6
Mr. Thomas Helsby	o	10	6
Mr. William Heywood	o	10	6
Mr. Thomas Hilton	o	10	6
Mr. William Heyward	o	10	6
Miss Sarah Harrison	o	10	6
Mr. Thomas Hethorn	o	7	o
Mrs. Thomas Haigh	o	7	o
Mr. Higginson	o	7	o
Mr. John Hadfield	o	7	o
Mr. T. Heywood	o	7	o
Mr. Richard Hartley	o	7	o
Mr. Richard Houghton	o	5	o
Mr. Thomas Hyde	o	5	o
Mr. James Heywood	o	5	o
Mr. Robert Hampson	o	5	o
Mr. John Hartley	o	5	o
Mr. William Hassall	o	5	o
Mr. Thomas Hopper	o	5	o
Mr. John Hudson	o	5	o
Mr. Peter Horsefield	o	5	o
Mr. Henry Hulme	o	5	o
Mr. James Holt	o	5	o
Mr. William Hyde	o	5	o
Mr. Hemingway	o	5	o

	£	s.	d.
Mr. Robert Hall	o	5	o
Mr. Richard Hannell	o	5	o
Mr. James Heywood	o	5	o
Mr. Heap	o	5	o
Mrs. Hardwick	o	5	o
Mr. Thomas Harding	o	5	o
Mr. Robert Heatley	o	5	o
Mr. Hutchinson	o	5	o
Mr. Charles Hague	o	5	o
Mr. John Hewetson	o	5	o
Mr. John Hindley	o	5	o

I & J

	£	s.	d.
Thomas Johnson, Esq.	5	5	o
Messrs. Jackson & Rushforth	2	2	o
Mr. William Jones	1	1	o
Messrs. William Joule & Co.	1	1	o
Mr. Thomas Johnson	1	1	o
Mr. Thomas Jackson	o	10	6
Mrs. Helen Joule	o	10	6
Mr. James Ingham	o	10	6
Messrs. James & Amies	o	10	6
Mr. Mathew Jepson	o	10	6
Mrs. Joynson	o	10	6
Mr. Aaron Jacob	o	10	6
Mr. Jepson	o	10	6
Mr. Thomas Jackson	o	10	o
Mr. John Irlam	o	7	o
Mr. T. Ingle	o	7	o
Mr. John Jennings	o	7	o
Mr. Luke Jackson	o	7	o
Mr. Jackson	o	7	7
Mr. James Inglish	o	7	o
Mr. John Jones	o	5	o
Mr. Thomas Jackson	o	5	o
Mr. Thomas Jones	o	5	o
Mr. Richard Jackson	o	5	o
Mr. Thomas Johnson	o	5	o
Mr. John Johnson	o	5	o
Messrs. M. & A. Johnson	o	5	o

	£	s.	d.
Mr. T. Johnson	o	5	o
Mr. Thomas Jenkins	o	5	o
Mr. River Jordan	o	5	o

K

	£	s.	d.
Mrs. Kirkman	1	1	o
Mr. Samuel Knight	1	1	o
Mr. James Kennedy	1	1	o
Mr. Thomas Kirkman	1	1	o
Mr. John Kenworthy	1	o	o
Mr. William Knowles	o	10	6
Mr. John Krauss	o	10	6
Mr. Stephen Kirk	o	7	o
Mr. John Krauss	o	7	o
Mr. Edward Kenyon	o	7	o
Mr. Peter Kerr	o	5	o
Mr. Abraham Kenyon	o	5	o
Mr. Thomas Kerr	o	5	o
Mr. John Kent	o	5	o
Mr. John Knight	o	5	o

L

	£	s.	d.
Mr. George Augustus Lee	2	2	o
Mr. Francis Larrard	1	1	o
Mess. Lamb, Lamb & Hobson	1	1	o
Mrs. Leeming	1	1	o
Mr. John Lyon	1	1	o
Mr. Joseph Lingard	1	1	o
Mr. Jerry Lees	1	1	o
Messrs. Litt & Co.	1	1	o
Mr. Thomas Livesey	1	1	o
Mr. David Locke	1	1	o
Mr. Joseph Lockett	1	1	o
Messrs. Law, Coates & Walker	1	1	o
Miss Layland	1	o	o
Mr. William Lane	1	o	o
Mr. James Lees	o	10	6
Mr. William Lamb	o	10	6

	£	s.	d.
Mr. Lallemande	o	10	6
Mr. Anthony Longsdon	o	10	6
Mr. William Lockett	o	10	6
Mr. William Lewis	o	10	6
Mr. Samuel Lockett	o	10	6
Mr. Robert Lucas	o	10	6
Mr. William Leaf	o	10	6
Mr. John Layland	o	10	6
Messrs. C. & N. Lings	o	10	6
Mr. William Lawson	o	10	6
Mr. William Lamb	o	10	6
Doctor Lignum	o	10	6
Mr. James Longworth	o	10	6
Mrs. Lightbourn	o	7	o
Mr. William Lazonby	o	7	o
Mr. Thomas Littlewood	o	7	o
Mr. George Lownds	o	7	o
Mr. John Lyon	o	7	o
Messrs. T. & M. Lang	o	7	o
Mr. Anthony Lane	o	5	o
Mrs. Lucy Leister	o	5	o
Mr. James Lowe	o	5	o
Mr. David Linch	o	5	o
Mr. George Lofthouse	o	5	o
Mr. Samuel Lees	o	5	o
Mrs. Lamb	o	5	o
Mr. Aaron Leech	o	5	o

M.

	£	s.	d.
Messrs. A. & G. Murray	3	3	o
Mr. Samuel Mottram	2	2	o
Mess. Mc.Connel & Kennedy	2	2	o
Messrs. Marsh, Reeve and Co.	2	2	o
Rev. R. Mashiter	1	1	o
Mr. Richard Methuan	1	1	o
Mr. John Mason	1	1	o
Mr. Joseph Mason	1	1	o
Mr. Charles Mc. Niven	1	1	o

	£	s.	d.
Mr. George Morton	1	1	o
Mr. F. M. Mallalieu.........	1	1	o
Mr. James Mollineux	1	1	o
Mr. Martin Marshall.........	1	1	o
Mr. Thomas Mort............	1	1	o
Mr. Thomas Mc. Dongal ...	1	1	o
Mr. William Marsden	1	1	o
Mr. John Marsden	1	1	o
Messrs. Milnes and Fowler	1	1	o
Mr. Thomas Marriott	1	1	o
Mr. Meritir.....................	1	o	o
Mr. Robert Moult............	1	o	o
Mr. George Merryweather..	o	10	6
Mr. Richard Mason	o	10	6
Mr. John Mc. Connel	o	10	6
Mrs. Sarah Mackey	o	10	6
Mr. Joseph Midwood	o	10	6
Mr. Mather	o	10	6
Mr. John Makin	o	10	6
Mr. Thomas Mather.........	o	10	6
Mr. Thomas Mellor	o	10	6
Mr. Matthias Morgan	o	10	6
Mr. Robert Mc. Clure	o	10	6
Mr. John Markendale	o	10	6
Mr. John Moon...............	o	10	6
Mr. Thomas Moverley	o	10	6
Mr. Henry Moult	o	10	6
Mr. Thomas Mather.........	o	10	6
Mrs. Susan Mottram...	o	10	6
Mrs. Peter Mc. Cormick ...	o	10	6
Mr. Nicholas Martindale ...	o	10	6
Mr. Andrew Mc. Kinzie ...	o	10	6
Messrs. Millward & Ravel..	o	10	6
Mr. John Malins	o	10	6
Mr. William Marston	o	10	6
Mr. William Maskell	o	10	6
Mr. Nathaniel Milne.........	o	10	6
Mr. John Marsden	o	10	6
Mr. George Magnus	o	10	6
Mr. Thomas Mottram	o	10	o

	£	s.	d.
Mr. Richard Moon	o	7	o
Mrs. Sarah Mackey	o	7	o
Mr. M. Malone	o	7	o
Mr. William Merryweather.	o	7	o
Mr. Samuel Malkin	o	7	o
Mr. Moses Malkin	o	7	o
Mr. Thomas Molineux	o	7	o
Mr. Robert Milnes	o	7	o
Mrs. Elizabeth Moore	o	7	o
Mr. William Moors	o	5	o
Mr. John Mills	o	5	o
Mr. Mansell	o	5	o
Mr. John Mc. Intejer	o	5	o
Mr. Isaac Martin	o	5	o
Mr. Isaac Mellor	o	5	o
Mr. William Morris	o	5	o
Mr. John Mc. Kinzie	o	5	o
Mr. Robert Mayers	o	5	o
Messrs. Mee & Co.	o	5	o
Mr. Thomas Mallalieu	o	5	o
Mr. John Mostyn	o	5	o
Mr. Abel Mosley	o	5	o
Mr. Joseph Makin............	o	5	o
Mr. William Marsh	o	5	o
Mr. Thomas Mellor	o	5	o

N.

	£	s.	d.
Miss Newberry	1	1	o
Messrs. Nanfan & Davis ...	1	1	o
Messrs. G. & J. Nedin......	1	1	o
Mr. William Norris	1	1	o
Mr. Joseph Nadin............	1	o	o
Mr. John Norman............	o	10	6
Mr. Needen	o	10	6
Mr. William Newall.........	o	10	6
Mr. Benjamin Nightingale.	o	10	6
Mrs. Norris	o	10	6
Mr. Thomas Nichols.........	o	10	6
Mr. Thomas Needen	o	10	6
Mr. John Norcliffe	o	10	6

	£	s.	d.
Mr. Martin Nelson	o	7	o
Mrs. Needham	o	7	o
Mr. Michael Noton	o	7	o
Mr. John Nield	o	5	o

O

	£	s.	d.
Mr. Richard Ormrod	2	2	o
Mr. John Orford	1	1	o
Mr. John Ollivant............	1	1	o
Mr. Richard Ormrod.........	1	o	o
Mr. Benjamin Oakden	1	o	o
Mr. William Occleshaw ...	o	10	6
Mr. Abraham Ogden	o	10	6
Mr. John Owen..............	o	10	6
Mr. Thomas Openshaw ...	o	10	6
Mrs. Ogden	o	5	o
Mr. William Olliver	o	5	o
Mr. James Oldfield	o	5	o
Mr. Andrew Olliver	o	5	o
Mr. Robert Oughton.........	o	5	o

P

	£	s.	d.
Messrs. S. Price and Co....	2	2	o
Mr. John Pooley, jun.	2	2	o
Mr. Jonathan Pollard	1	1	o
Mr. Alexander Patterson ...	1	1	o
Messrs. Peel, Williams and Co.	1	1	.
Messrs. T. and M. Pickford	1	1	o
Messrs. Robert Parker and Co.	1	1	o
Messrs. Phillips and Elliott.	1	1	o
Messrs. Thos. and Rich. Potter	1	1	o
Mr. James Preston	1	1	o
Mr. John Pooley, sen.	1	1	o
Mr. James Poulson	1	1	o
Mr. T. Preston	1	1	o
Mrs. Pickup	1	1	o
Mr. Robert Peel	1	1	o

	£	s.	d.
Mrs. Elizabeth Pennington.	1	1	o
Mr. W. Pendleton............	o	10	6
Mrs. Elizabeth Pointon......	o	10	6
Mr. John Pickford............	o	10	6
Mr. Charles Payant	o	10	6
Mr. Gerrard Pendlebury ...	o	10	6
Mr. Robert Prescot	o	10	6
Mrs. Mary Pollitt	o	10	5
Mr. Ralph Prince	o	10	6
Messrs. A. Preston and Co.	o	10	6
Mr. Thomas Parry	o	10	6
Mr. Thomas Potter	o	10	6
Mr. Francis Pickering	o	10	6
Messrs. Priestnall & Booth.	o	10	6
Mr. Adam Parkinson	o	10	5
Mr. George Pratt	o	10	6
Mr. William Paul	o	10	6
Mr. George Palfreyman ...	o	10	6
Mrs. Pilling	o	10	o
Mr. Samuel Popplewell ...	o	7	o
Mr. Isaac Pickstock	o	7	o
Mr. James Platford	o	7	o
Mrs. Pearson..................	o	7	o
Mrs. Sarah Pollitt............	o	5	o
Mr. John Pickford............	o	5	o
Mr. Pape	o	5	o
Mr. Serjeant Porter	o	5	o
Mrs. Mary Pemberton	o	5	o
Mrs. Joseph Partington ...	o	5	o
Mr. James Pendleton	o	5	o
Mr. Thomas Powell.........	o	5	o
Mr. Robert Parker	o	5	o
Mrs. Pennington	o	5	o

R

	£	s.	d.
Mr. John Rigg	1	1	o
Mr. Thomas Rawlinson ...	1	1	o
Mrs. Runcorn	1	1	o
Mess. Radford & Wadding-ton	1	1	o

	£	s.	d.
Mrs. Martha Rexford	1	1	0
Mr. Jeremiah Royle	1	1	0
Mr. William Renshaw	1	1	0
Mr. Wilson Rigg	1	1	0
Mr. Charles Rickards	1	1	0
Mr. William Russell	1	1	0
Mr. Samuel Russell	1	1	0
Mr. John Rolinson	1	1	0
Mr. James Rothwell	1	1	0
Mr. Richards	1	0	0
Mess. Rimmer & Wainhouse	0	10	6
Mr. Richardson	0	10	6
Mr. George Rutherford	0	10	6
Messrs. Robertson & Ingle.	0	10	6
Mr. Joseph Richards	0	10	6
Mr. Charles Rowland	0	10	6
Mr. Joseph Rothwell	0	10	6
Mr. John Radcliffe	0	10	6
Mr. Joshua Ryle	0	10	6
Mr. William Raby	0	10	6
Mr. Micah Rose	0	10	6
Mrs. Lydia Richardson	0	10	6
Rev. Robinson Eldsdale	0	10	6
Mr. John Redhead	0	10	6
Mr. John Ramsbotham	0	10	6
Mr. Richard Richardson	0	10	6
Mr. William Roberts	0	7	0
Mr. Peter Rock	0	5	0
Mr. Thomas Rooker	0	5	0
Mr. William Reynolds	0	5	0
Mrs. Elizabeth Rowe	0	5	0
Mr. Thomas Robinson	0	5	0
Mrs. Elizabeth Redford	0	5	0
Mr. John Royle	0	5	0
Mr. James Rose	0	5	0
Mr. John Rider	0	5	0
Mr. John Robinson	0	5	0

S

	£	s.	d.
Rev. Thomas Stone	1	1	0
Rev. Jeremiah Smith	1	1	0

	£	s.	d.
Mr. John Sherratt	1	1	0
Mr. William Sherratt	1	1	0
Mr. Thomas Sherratt	1	1	0
Mr. Thomas Slack	1	1	0
Mr. Stocks	1	1	0
Mr. T. W. Smith	1	1	0
Messrs. B. & W. Sandford.	1	1	0
Mr. Robert Slack	1	1	0
Mr. John Sutton	1	1	0
Mr. Joseph Sutton	1	1	0
Messrs. Shikelthorp and Thomason	1	1	0
Messrs. N. Shelmerdine & Co.	1	1	0
Messrs. Scatchard & Hardy	1	1	0
Mr. Thomas Salter	1	1	0
Mr. T. R. Sanders	1	1	0
Mr. John Shaw	1	1	0
Mr. Thomas Slater	1	1	0
Mr. Thomas Sefton	1	1	0
Mr. John Stephenson	1	1	0
Mr. William Sergent	1	1	0
Mr. John Singleton	1	1	0
Mr. Alexander Smith	1	1	0
Mr. William Shankland	0	10	6
Mr. Robert Schofield	0	10	6
Mr. John Smith	0	10	6
Mrs. Stevenson	0	10	6
Messrs. Salt and Walker	0	10	6
Mr. Thomas Walt	0	10	6
Mr. Thomas Scholes	0	10	6
Mr. John Spencer	0	10	6
Mr. John Sevill	0	10	6
Mr. John Shaw	0	10	6
Mr. John Scholes	0	10	6
Mr. William Sudlow	0	10	6
Messrs. S. & E. Deavill	0	10	6
Mr. John Sykes	0	10	6
Mr. William Seedhouse	0	10	6
Mr. Robert Scarr	0	10	6

L

	£	s.	d.
Mrs. Ann Stephens	0	10	6
Mr. Sattersfield	0	10	6
Mr. James Smith	0	10	6
Mr. Thomas Staines	0	10	6
Mrs. Alice Schofield	0	10	6
Mr. Richard Salter	0	10	6
Mr. John Sterrup	0	10	6
Messrs. Sterndale & Robley	0	10	6
Mr. Joseph Stelfox	0	10	6
Mrs. Elizabeth Stubbs	0	10	6
Mr. William Sumner	0	10	6
Mr. W. T. Simpson	0	10	6
Mr. George Smith	0	10	6
Mrs. Jane Shore	0	10	6
Mr. Joseph Seddon	0	10	6
Mr. Richard Shires	0	10	6
Mr. Thomas Smith	0	10	0
Mr. John Smith	0	7	0
Mr. George Stringer	0	7	0
Mr. John Stanfield	0	7	0
Mrs. Hannah Smith	0	7	0
Miss Schofield	0	7	0
Mr. Ferdinand Swengley	0	7	0
Mr. Robert Saxon	0	7	0
Mr. John Smith	0	7	0
Mr. S. Sidebottom	0	7	0
Mr. W. Shaw	0	7	0
Mr. Jacob Sevill	0	7	0
Mr. Phineas Sykes	0	7	0
Mr. John Shankland	0	5	0
Mr. James Standring	0	5	0
Mr. Samuel Slater	0	5	0
Mr. James Slater	0	5	0
Mr. Thomas Sykes	0	5	0
Mr. Thomas Slack	0	5	0
Mr. Thruston Smethurst	0	5	0
Mr. Joseph Slater	0	5	0
Mr. Joseph Standring	0	5	0
Mr. Joseph Slater	0	5	0
Mr. Thomas Stanfield	0	5	0

	£	s.	d.
Mr. Daniel Smith	0	5	0
Mr. William Stoby	0	5	0
Mr. John Stringer	0	5	0
Mr. Michael Satterthwaite	0	5	0
Mr. Thomas Swanwick	0	5	0
Mr. John Salmon	0	5	0
Mr. John Southerby	0	5	0
Messrs. Staines & Mottershead	0	5	0
Mr. John Speed	0	5	0
Mr. Josiah Saxton	0	5	0
Mr. Matthew Steele	0	5	0

T

	£	s.	d.
Mr. James Taylor	1	1	0
Messrs. W. & E. Turner	1	1	0
Messrs. T. & W. Tetlow	1	1	0
Mr. William Townend	1	1	0
Mr. Thomas Tebbutt	1	1	0
Mr. Richard Tonge	1	1	0
Mr. J. Taylor	1	0	0
Mr. William Tate	1	0	0
Mr. Joseph Thorley	0	10	6
Mr. John Thornber	0	10	6
Mr. John Taylor	0	10	6
Mr. Peter Tuer	0	10	6
Messrs. J. & J. Taylor	0	10	6
Mr. John Trible	0	10	6
Mr. J. Thompson	0	10	6
Mrs. Jane Taylor	0	10	6
Mr. Thomas Taylor	0	10	6
Mrs. Thorpe	0	10	6
Mr. William Tattersall	0	10	6
Mr. William Tuer	0	10	6
Mr. John Travis	0	10	6
Mr. William Tyson	0	10	6
Mr. Josiah Twyford	0	10	6
Mr. George Teale	0	10	6
Mr. John Thompson	0	10	6
Mr. Richard Turner	0	10	6

	£	s.	d.
Mr. William Tysic	o	7	o
Mr. Tomlinson	o	7	o
Mr. John Travis	o	7	o
Mr. Thompson	o	7	o
Mr. Tattersall	o	5	o
Mr. James Taylor	o	5	o
Mr. John Thompson	o	5	o
Mr. Thomas Thornley	o	5	o
Mr. John Tute	o	5	o
Mr. Robert Tinker	o	5	o
Mr. John Taylor	o	5	o
Mrs. Taylor	o	5	o
Mr. J. Thompson	o	5	o
Mr. John Tomlinson	o	5	o
Mr. George Tengatt	o	5	o
Mr. Thomas Taylor	o	5	o

U & V

	£	s.	d.
Messrs. B. Uhde & Co.	1	1	o
Mr. Nathaniel Underwood.	o	10	6
Mr. Vernon Underwood	o	5	o
Mr. George Vickers	1	1	o
Mr. William Vickers	o	10	6
Mr. George Vaughan	o	5	o

W

	£	s.	d.
Messrs. Worthington, Baxter and Co.	3	3	o
Mr. George Walker	3	3	o
Mr. Thomas Whitelegg	1	1	o
Messrs. J. &. J. Wright	1	1	o
Messrs. William Wright & Co.	1	1	o
Mr. John Whitehead	1	1	o
Mrs. Walker	1	1	o
Mr. William Wright	1	1	o
Mr. John Whitehead	1	1	o
Mr. Jeremiah Whittenbury.	1	1	o
Mr. John Whitehead	1	1	o
Messrs. C. Wheeler & Son.	1	1	o
Mr. Charles White	1	1	o

	£	s.	d.
Mr. John Waller	1	1	o
Mr. William Wright	1	1	o
Mrs. Winter	1	1	o
Mr. John Walker	1	1	o
Mr. Benjamin Williams	1	1	o
Mr. Thomas Williams	1	1	o
Mr. Benjamin Wilson	1	1	o
Mr. Jonathan Warren	1	o	o
Mr. Edward Weaver	o	10	6
Mr. John Walker	o	10	6
Mrs. Alice Withington	o	10	6
Messrs. J. & T. Watts	o	10	6
Mr John Walker	o	10	6
Mr. Henry Wilmot	o	10	6
Miss Whitlow	o	10	6
Mr. James Withnall	o	10	6
Mr. James Wright	o	10	6
Mr. Job Wragg	o	10	6
Mr. John White	o	10	6
Messrs. B. E. & J. Wilson.	o	10	6
Mr. William Waltham	o	10	6
Mr. Joseph Wells	o	10	6
Mr. Phillip Withington	o	10	6
Mr. Christopher Weatherall	o	10	6
Mr. Williams	o	10	6
Mr. Samuel Walker	o	10	6
Mr. John Wooley	o	10	6
Messrs. W. Wright & Son.	o	10	6
Mr. Edward Wright	o	10	6
Mr. John Whitehead	o	10	6
Mr. Robert Whitby	o	10	6
Messrs. Wood & Westhead.	o	10	6
Mr. James Walley	o	10	6
Mr. Thomas Whittaker	o	10	6
Mr. Henry Wood	o	10	6
Messrs. Wells & Walker	o	10	6
Mr. Samuel Williamson	o	10	6
Mr. Thomas Walker	o	10	6
Mr. Samuel Walker	o	10	6
Mr. James Wrigley	o	10	6

	£	s.	d.
Mr. William Woodhouse ...	0	10	6
Mr. Thomas Woodburn ...	0	10	6
Mr. John Wilson	0	10	6
Mr. Samuel Wilcock.........	0	10	6
Rev. R. H. Whitelock......	0	10	6
Mr. John Whitehead.........	0	10	6
Mr. Samuel Worthington ..	0	10	6
Mrs. Sarah Worrall	0	10	6
Mrs. Mary Wilson......... ...	0	10	6
Mr. Job Wragg............ ..	0	10	6
Mr. Whittaker	0	10	6
Mr. Benjamin Wrigley......	0	10	0
Mr. John White...............	0	7	6
Mr. William Wood	0	7	0
Mr. James Woodburne......	0	7	0
Mr. Thomas Ward	0	7	0
Mr. James Warren	0	7	0
Mr. William Willetts	0	7	0
Mr. Richard Wormald......	0	7	0
Mr. Samuel Wade............	0	7	0
Mr. James Welsh	0	6	0
Mrs. Martha Waite	0	5	0
Mr. Peter Williams	0	5	0

	£	s.	d.
Mr. Henry Wilson	0	5	0
Mr. Richard Wilson.........	0	5	0
Mr. Charles Worrall.........	0	5	0
Mrs. Walker	0	5	0
Mr. Thomas Wainwright...	0	5	0
Mr. Francis Woodiwiss......	0	5	0
Mr. John Winder	0	5	0
Mr. Wiggins	0	5	0
Mr. Christopher Wederburn	0	5	0
Mr. S. Wood..................	0	5	0
Mr. William Wood	0	5	0
Mr. Josiah Wolstencroft ...	0	5	0
Mr. John Walker	0	5	0
Mr. Western	0	5	0
Mr. Witlow	0	5	0
Mr. H. Walker......	0	5	0

Y

	£	s.	d.
Mr. Joseph Young	0	10	6
Mr. Joseph Yates	0	10	6
Mr. John Yates	0	7	0
Amount of Subscriptions *under* five shillings	24	3	9

Those who are disposed to contribute to this Charity, by their last Will,
are desired to do it in the following Terms :

"I give and bequeath unto A. B. and C. D. the sum of
in Trust, that they pay the same to the Treasurer of a Society, who call
themselves Trustees of the Public SUNDAY SCHOOLS in Manchester and
Salford, belonging to the Established Church ; which sum I desire may be
paid out of my PERSONAL Estate, and applied to the use of the said Charity."

The present State and Mode of Conducting the Sunday Schools in Manchester and Salford under the Establishment.

Collectors.	Districts.	No. of the School, and where situated.	Gentlemen Visitors.	Masters and Mistresses.	Number of Assistants.	Boys	Girls.	Total
Mr. Wm. Hutchinson, Mr. George Neden, Mr. James Withnall, Mr. Joshua Royle, Mr. John Bingham, Rev. M. Randall.	No. 1. Collegiate Church.	Fennel-street	Rev. C. D. Wray, A.M., Mr. William Wright, Mr. James Withnall, Mr. Thomas Garnett.	William Fall, John Caldwell	One.	102	157	259
Mr. John Ollivant, Mr. Micah Rose, Mr. R. Howarth, Mr. Holford.	No. 2. St. Ann's.	1 & 2 Tib Lane.	Rev. M. Randall, B.A., Mr. John Johnson, Mr. John Holford, Mr. Josiah Twyford.	William Taylor	Three.	46	81	127
Mr. Robert Ryder, Mr. William Bowman, Mr. Samuel Brett, Mr. W. T. Simpson.	No. 3. St. Mary's.	1 & 2 Star Yard.	Rev. J. Gatliff, A.M., Mr. William Bowman, Mr. Samuel Brett, Mr. W. T. Simpson.	John Amery, Henry Holt	Six.	120	140	260
Rev. R. Mashiter, Mr. John Kenedy, Mr. Thomas Whitelegg, Mr. John Pollard, Mr. Thomas Slack, Mr. Robert Slack, Mr. William Fell, Mr. T. Worthington, Mr. John Sutton, Mr. Thomas Markland, Mr. Jos. Mills, Mr. T. Ingle, Mr. William Aspell, Mr. Richard Cundell, Mr. Taylor, Mr. Todd.	No. 4. St. Paul's.	1 Gun-street	Rev. Thos. Whitelegg, Mr. Thomas Markland, Mr. James Taylor, Mr. Young, Mr. James Taylor, jun.	William Stonehewer, Elizabeth Wallace	Five.	113	107	220
		2 Turner-street	Rev. R. Mashiter, Mr. Thomas Markland, Mr. B. G. Mashiter, Mr. James Taylor, Mr. Thomas Slack.	John Howgote, William Howarth	Five.	132	116	248
		3 Silk-street	Rev. R. Mashiter, Mr. Wm. Aspell, Mr. Timothy Ingle, Mr. James Mills.	William Gradwell, Samuel Bloomley, William Birch, George Horner	Five.	100	143	243
		4 Jersey-street	Rev. R. Mashiter, Mr. Thomas Whitelegg, Mr. Carr, Mr. James Taylor, Mr. Thomas Slack.	John Young	Nineteen.	339	345	684
		5 George Leigh-street	Rev. R. Mashiter, Mr. Thomas Whitelegg, Mr. Thomas Slack.	David Stott	Forty.	672	854	1526

Mode of Conducting the Sunday Schools in Manchester and Salford—Continued.

Collectors.	Districts.	No. of the School, and where situated.	Gentlemen Visitors.	Masters and Mistresses.	Number of Assistants.	Boys	Girls	Total
Mr. Robert Chadwick, Mr. Thomas Tebbutt, Mr. Peter Fletcher, Mr. Edward Woollam	No. 5. *St. John's.*	1 St. John's	Rev. J. Clowes, M.A., Mr. John Ollivant, Mr. Wm. Hutchinson, Mr. T. S. Fogg, Mr. Thomas Fleming, Mr. Wm. Butterworth, Mr. William Lockett, Mr. John Hodson, Mr. Joseph Gleave, Mr. Charles Gee, Mr. John Whittaker, Mr. George Morton, Mr. J. R. Stevenson, Mr. Thomas Atherton, Mr. Thomas Garnett	James Morton, Ann Powell, Sarah Hassall, Sarah Haworth	Eight & half.	210	330	540
Mr. William Wright, Mr. John Waller, Mr. Henry Burgess, Mr. Wilson Rigg, Mr. Thomas Moverley	No. 6. *St. James's.*	1 & 2 Portland-street	Rev. C. Bailey, D.D., Mr. William Wright, Mr. Henry Burgess, Mr. Thomas Moverley, Mr. John Pickup, Mr. John Waller, Mr. Wilson Rigg	Joseph Fearnhead, Esther Stevenson	Six.	200	220	420
Mr. Edward Clegg, Mr. John Barlow, Mr. S. Mather, Mr. John Sevill, Mr. Bond, Mr. Thomas Scholes	No. 7. *St. Michael's.*	1 & 2 Millers-street	Rev. M. Wrigley, A.M., Mr. Edward Clegg, Mr. John Barlow, Mr. John Sevill, Mr. Thomas Mather, Mr. Thomas Scholes	John Bryan, Joseph Jones	Twelve.	330	440	770
Mr. James Braddock, Mr. William Cooper, jun., Mr. Thomas Jackson, Mr. John Brown	No. 8. *St. Peter's*	1 Jackson's Row	Rev. S. Hall, A.M., Mr. James Braddock, Mr. Samuel Livsey	Thomas Richardson, James Lowe	Seven.	269	146	415
		2 Alport Town	Rev. S. Hall, A.M., Mr. Robert Howarth, Mr. William Cooper	Hassal Parker	Five & half.	180	160	340

Mode of Conducting the Sunday Schools in Manchester and Salford—Continued.

Collectors.	Districts.	No. of the School, and where situated.	Gentlemen Visitors.	Masters and Mistresses.	Number of Assistants.	Boys	Girls	Total
Mr. George Walker, Mr. Abraham Ogden, Mr. Charles Rowland, Mr. John Hogarth, Mr. Hardy, Mr. John Hurst	No. 9. Trinity.	1 Workhouse	Rev. Mr. Clowes, Mr. George Walker, Mr. Martin Clayton, Mr. John Aspinwall	William Taylor, Hannah Shuttleworth	Four.	112	117	229
		2 King's Head Yard	Rev. Mr. Clowes, Mr. Abraham Ogden, Mr. Thomas Helsby, Mr. William Cowdroy, Mr. John Ryder	John Stanley	Five.	94	110	204
Rev. E. Booth, Mr. George Gould, Mr. Samuel Mottram, Mr. N. Shelmerdine, Mr. James Hall, jun., Mr. D. Locke, Mr. Samuel Walker	No. 10. St. Stephen's.	1 Bloom-street	Rev. E. Booth, N. Gould, Esq., Mr. T. O. Gill, Mr. Samuel Mottram, Mr. N. Shelmerdine, Mr. Joseph Poole, Mr. Joseph Lockett, Mr. Thomas Garnett, Mr. Thos. Shelmerdine, Mr. Richard Gould, Mr. Charles Fearne, Mr. F. Ridings, Mr. George Vickers, Mr. Joseph Hall, Mr. Joseph Gaskin	Robert Needham	Five.	299	298	597
		2 Oldfield Lane	Rev. E. Booth, Mr. George Gould, Mr. Spencer	William Brierley	Five.	145	197	342
						3465	3961	7424

General Visitors.

Nathaniel Gould, Esq.
Mr. T. O. Gill.
Mr. Thomas Whitelegg.
Mr. John Ollivant.
Mr. William Hutchinson.

Lady Visitors.

St. Mary's...... Mrs. Brett.
St. John's... { Miss Holford. Miss B. Green. Mrs. Sandford. Miss Byrom.

Lady Visitors.

St. John's.... { Mrs. Marshall. Mrs. Ollivant.
St. Michael's.. { Mrs. Clegg. Mrs. Barlow.
No. 2. { Miss Ann Spencer.
St. Stephen's... { Miss Mary Winterbottom. Miss Mary Brotherton.

The Singing in the above Schools conducted by Mr. John Bond.

APPENDIX III.

MANCHESTER HYMN BOOKS.

IN my chapter on Archdeacon Ward's curates, I have incidentally made mention of a compilation, entitled "Select Portions of Dr. Brady's and Mr. Tate's Version of the Psalms; together with a few selected from the Old Version. Also a Collection of Hymns and Sanctuses for the use of St. Ann's Church, Manchester. 'Let the Word of Christ dwell in you richly in all wisdom; teaching and admonishing one another in psalms, and hymns, and spiritual songs; singing with grace in your heart to the Lord.'—To be had of J. Kay, clerk, only. Manchester: Printed by C. Wheeler: 1784."

The compilation of this Hymn Book, I have already shown to be Mr. Hall's work. Milton's lines—

> Now let the pealing organ blow,
> To the full voic'd choir below,
> In service high, and anthems clear,
> As may, with sweetness through mine ear,
> Dissolve me into extacies,
> And bring all heaven before mine eyes.

which are set before the Hymns and Sanctuses, would naturally be his selection.

It may be well to add a few words about some of the local Hymn Books that followed. Through the kindness of Mr. John Scholes I have received a copy of what I suppose would be considered a second edition of the selection above mentioned. The title page is the same, saving that the date 1790 takes the place of 1784. The note at the end of the book (*vide* p. 103)—stating that the Ardwick collection is identical with this, and that all the hymns used at St. John's and St. Paul's (two distinct compilations) are found in the same, and that by following the directions set down the St. Ann's collection can be used at either of these two places of worship,—is to be seen unaltered in this second edition. From this it is manifest that while St. John's and St. Paul's used different selections, all three Hymn Books were published in concert, and were local productions. I am sorry to say I have not as yet met with a copy of the other Hymn Books in question.

The next local compilation seems to have been the work of the Rev. Edward Smyth, who in the Directory for 1815 is set down as "Minister of St. Clements," and living at "Chorlton Hall." This Hymn Book is styled "A Collection of Hymns, Psalms, and Anthems, designed for the congregation attending St. Clement's Chapel, Manchester. By the Rev. Edward Smyth. 'Be filled with the Spirit, speaking to yourselves in Psalms, and Hymns, and spiritual Songs, singing and making melody in your hearts to the Lord.' Eph. v. 18-19—Col. iii. 16. 'Is any merry? let him sing Psalms.' James v. 13. Soliti essent Christiani, stato die, convenire, carmen-que Christo, quasi Deo, dicere secum invicem. Plin. Ep. Lib.: Jo Ep. 97. Manchester: Printed by Sowler and Russell, MDCCXCIII." This is a much larger and more pretentious compilation than Mr. Hall's; it contains 263 hymns, in which some of the "Brady and Tate" psalms are included; St. Ann's book has but 103. It is more carefully put together; the subject of the verses below stands at the top of every page. There is a table of "General Contents," as well as an "Index of First Lines;" both these are wanting in the earlier collection. There is also a complete "book of words" of the "Messiah" appended, one more proof, if proof were necessary, how popular in Lancashire and Yorkshire had this Oratorio become at the close of the last century. A selection from Handel's great work was the favoured treat allowed the singers on all such important occasions as the Charity Collection or the Sunday School Anniversary. Mr. Bennett, rector of St. Mary's, when preaching for the latter institution at Hindley, near Wigan, in 1786, actually took his choir with him to aid the local talent; the advertisement announcing a selection from the Messiah as part of the proceedings.

Probably the most interesting feature of Mr. Smyth's collection is found in the hymns (evidently of local inspiration), "for Fast Days and in times of National Trouble." They all bear reference to the prevailing wars and rumours of wars. Allusions to national vices and "Tophet" abound.   Hymn CCLX. begins—

> O God, the great, the fearful God,
> To Thee we humbly sue for peace :
> Groaning beneath a nation's load,
> And crushed by our own wickedness,
> Our guilt we tremble to declare,
> And pour out our sad souls in prayer.
>
> Both rich and poor, both high and low,
> Have trampled on Thy mild command :
> The floods of wickedness o'erflow,
> And deluge our apostate land :
> People and priests lie drown'd in sin,
> And Tophet yawns to take us in.

The next thus sets out in an equally penitentiary spirit—

> Jesu, sin-atoning Lamb,
>   Thine utmost pity show !
> All the virtues of Thy name,
>   Oh, let Thy rebels know !
> Tophet is our just reward,
> Yet snatch us from the burning lake—
> Spare the guilty nation, Lord,
>   For Thine own mercy's sake.

The refrain of every verse in this hymn, which has decided
merit from a poetical point of view, is—

> Spare the guilty nation, Lord,
> For Thine own mercy's sake.

It is well known that there was a great fear of a French invasion at this time. Evidently the good folk in Manchester
were alarmed. Several hymns bear direct allusion to such a
possibility. The same hymn concludes—

> Oh, alarm the sleeping crowd
> And fill their souls with dread !
> Then avert the lowering cloud,
> Impending o'er our head !
> Turn aside th' invading sword,
> And drive the alien armies back—
> Spare the guilty nation, Lord,
> For Thine own mercy's sake.

Hymn CCLXII. is also creditable to the writer ; nevertheless, it
is marked by a very terror-stricken spirit, and did we not know
that Manchester turned out some splendid corps of volunteers
at this time, men who were wont to " keep their powder dry,"
we might be disposed to think these hymns inspired rather by
a craven dread of the foreign invader than a fear of God's
righteous judgments upon our national sins. This begins thus :

> Dreadful sin-chastening God,
> If Thy decree be past—
> If the long-impending rod
> Must scourge our land at last,

The next is like to it—

> Ah, whither should we fly,
> In peril and distress,
> While all the dogs of war are nigh,
> The enemies of peace ?
> Almighty God of love,
> On Thee our souls we cast,
> Oh, send deliv'rance from above,
> And save our land at last !

A leopard watches o'er
  Our cities night and day,
Prepar'd with unrelenting pow'r
  To swallow up his prey :
The alien armies wait,
  Lured by the scent of blood,
As awful ministers of fate—
  As thunderbolts of God.

Yet if our sin demands,
  Its just reward of pain,
Oh, let us fall into the hands
  Of God, and not of man !
His tender mercies wound,
  Remorseless as the grave ;
But pity in Thy wrath is found,
  Which only strikes to save.

In measure, then, reprove—
  In love Thine own chastise :
But baffle, and far off remove
  Our threatening enemies :
Blast their devices, Lord,
  Nor let their counsel stand—
Knap Thou the spear, and break the sword,
  Of all the hostile band.

Hymn CCLVIII. was manifestly written for a fast day. There
had been several in the few years preceding its publication
(1793). The fifth verse runs as follows—

We now of fleets, and armies vaunt,
  And ships and men prepare :
But men like Moses most we want,
  To save the state by prayer.

Yet, Lord, we hope Thou hast prepared,
  A hidden few to-day,
(The nation's secret strength and guard),
  To weep, and mourn, and pray.

Nothing could be more interesting, had we time and space
to spare, to trace the connection between the publication of

these hymns (St. Clement's was opened for divine service on Christmas Day, 1793, and the Hymn Book was printed for use from that date) and the great commercial and political depression which had reigned over Manchester throughout that same year. Men who had been growing rich were growing poor again, gaunt famine brooded over the land, and it was hard for the poor to obtain the barest necessities of life. A spirit of rebellion was, or was supposed to be, rampant in the land. Within two months of the publication of these hymns Thomas Walker, the late boroughreeve, and Mr. Collier were tried at the Lancaster Assizes on the charge of having conspired to overthrow the constitution, and assist the French in the threatened attack upon this island. They were acquitted, however, and returned to Manchester in triumph. Nevertheless, the incident serves to show what a terrible panic was abroad on the subject of a French invasion, and explains the piteous and almost abject terror that fills this local and contemporaneous publication. Strange we should find a history of English political sentiment in a hymn book !

The last local compilation of this kind I would notice is Mr. Hall's, published in 1809. Mr. Hall died September 22, 1713, and from the year 1794 was rector of St. Peter's. We can understand that he would wish his new church to adopt a service book which he had himself drawn up, and which had been in use in a neighbouring sanctuary for the past ten years. Evidently he very soon set about re-arranging his first work. He omitted some Psalms ; he added a large number of other and newer hymns; and in 1809 sent forth this his second hymn book, although it must really be considered but a third edition of that printed in 1784 and 1790. The title-page is virtually the same. " For the use of St. Ann's Church, Manchester" is altered to "for the use of St. Ann's and St. Peter's Churches, Manchester." "To be had of J. Kay, clerk, only," is also wanting. The publisher is not, this time, C. Wheeler. "Printed and sold by

M. Bancks, corner of St. Ann's Square, 1809." That St. Ann's
and St. Peter's should use such a book is quite natural. The
new church had taken a large slice of the district attached to
the older one ; the rector of St. Peter's had been curate of St.
Ann's ; the rector of St. Ann's (Rev. Robert Barker) had most
probably, as already stated, been curate of the same church in
1779. Thus the publication of the hymn book of 1809, for
use in both churches, was only cementing a connection which
had existed between the two rectors for at least thirty years.

Hymn XLIV. looks very like a composition we should expect
from the pen of Mr. Hall—

> Let Avarice from shore to shore
> Her fav'rite god pursue :
> Thy word, O Lord, we value more
> Than India or Peru.

What a change of tone in the special appendix of 1809 from
that of 1793 ! France had not invaded England ; the Battle of
the Nile had been fought and won ; Trafalgar and Nelson had
astonished the world ; the Duke of Gloucester had inspected
and praised 6,000 Manchester Volunteers at Ardwick in 1804.
Mr. Hall was chaplain to the first battalion. Doubtless
Hymn III. in the appendix was written for the General Thanksgiving of December 5, 1805—

> To Thee, who reign'st supreme above
> And reign'st supreme below,
> Thou God of wisdom, power, and love,
> We our successes owe.
>
> The thundering horse, the martial band,
> Without thine aid were vain :
> And victory flies at thy command
> To crown the bright campaign :
>
> Thy mighty arm, unseen, was nigh,
> When we our foes assailed :
> 'Tis Thou hast raised our honors high,
> And o'er their foes prevailed.

What though no columns lifted high
   Stand deep inscribed with praise,
Yet sounding honours to the sky,
   Our grateful tongues shall raise.

To our young race will we proclaim
   The mercies God has shown :
That they may learn to bless His name,
   And choose Him for their own.

Thus, while we sleep in silent dust,
   When threatening dangers come,
Their fathers' God shall be their trust
   Their refuge, and their home.

If bad trade made Manchester men penitential in 1790, they were grateful for an improvement. Hymn IV. verse 4 says (evidently written for 1802, "the year of peace and plenty")—

Then Peace returns with balmy wing
   (Sweet peace ! with her what blessings fled :)
Glad plenty laughs, the vallies sing
   Reviving Commerce lifts her head.

INDEX.

M

CPSIA information can be obtained at www.ICGtesting.com
Printed in the USA
241688LV00002B/19/P